THE
HISTORY AND ANTIQUITIES

OF

EYAM;

WITH A FULL AND PARTICULAR ACCOUNT OF THE

GREAT PLAGUE,

WHICH DESOLATED THAT VILLAGE.

A.D. 1666.

BY WILLIAM WOOD.

' Some writer,—why I know not,—has styled this ancient village the Queen of
the Peak. If it be so, alas, she is indeed a widowed one ! for there she
stands alone among the hills, the solemn monument of 'A MIGHTY
WOE,' that still tingles appallingly in the ear of history, and embues the
whole district with a spirit of pensive gloom."
RAMBLES IN THE COUNTRY.

LONDON:
THOMAS MILLER, NEWGATE STREET; SHEFFIELD, A. WHITAKER;
CHESTERFIELD, J. ATKINSON; BAKEWELL, J. GOODWIN;
AND THE AUTHOR, EYAM.

1842.
PRICE THREE SHILLINGS.

DEDICATION.

———

TO HIS GRACE THE DUKE OF DEVONSHIRE,

TO HIS GRACE THE DUKE OF BUCKINGHAM,

AND

TO HIS LORDSHIP THE EARL OF THANET,

LORDS OF THE MANOR OF EYAM,

THIS UNASSUMING, LITTLE VOLUME,

IS MOST HUMBLY

AND GRATEFULLY

DEDICATED,

BY THE

AUTHOR.

PREFACE.

COUNTRY villages, in a great measure, afford but few circumstances sufficiently important for historical compilation: indeed, general interest cannot be excited by occurrences of a purely local character ; and, therefore, all histories of small places, divested of imaginary incidents, must be strictly confined to the notice of their respective inhabitants. A well-written history of Eyam, a sequestered village in the Peak, would, however, be well worthy of public perusal: this "little mountain city"——being "overshadowed by the spirit of old"—hallowed by the ever-present *shades* of the greatest of moral heroes—encircled with an enduring and a dazzling halo of genius, must ever render it a place of deep, general, and intense interest.

The awful circumstance connected with the local history of this romantic village—its desolation by the plague A.D. 1666,—has, from its occurrence, strongly elicited the attention and notice of a great portion of the sympathizing and thinking public. This may be inferred from the calamitous event having at sundry times called into action the highly classic pens of the following elegant authors :—Dr. Mead, Miss Anna Seward, Allan Cunningham, E. Rhodes, S. T. Hall, William and Mary Howitt, S. Roberts, J. Holland, and a many others, who have, in verse and prose, laudably endeavoured to perpetuate the sufferings of a joint number of mortals, who, like Codrus and Curtius, offered themselves up a self-sacrifice for the salvation of their country.

Highly commendable as are the brief descriptions of these illustrious authors, on this painfully interesting subject, they are, however, respectively deficient in ample detail,—in correct data,—in the enumeration of material circumstances, —and in being compiled from cursory, casual, and erroneous information: defects, which could have been avoided only by a long residence in the locality. To rectify the mistakes of preceding writers,—to introduce many hitherto omitted circumstances,—to snatch almost from oblivion a great number of incidents,—to collect into one body all the available information connected with that direful visitation, has been my humble attempt; and to whatever degree I may have succeeded, it must not be ascribed to paramount intellectual ability; but solely to having invariably resided amongst the

impressive memorials of that awful scourge. Thus circum-
stanced I have also had the advantage of hearing, a thousand
times repeated, all the many traditions on that doleful
subject.

It is to be regretted that a minute account of the occurrence was not taken nearer the time: and I cannot but sincerely wish, that the task had fallen into far more able hands
even now.

The principal part of the following work has already been
before the public in a series of chapters, published a few
months ago in the *Sheffield Iris*. To the proprietors of that
highly literary and liberal paper, I feel the most grateful sense
of obligation. And the obliging favours of a few other inestimable friends are fully and justly appreciated, if here but
briefly acknowledged.

An engraving of Cucklet Church, Mompesson's Well,
Riley-graves, the Cross, and the Church, would be a great
and pleasing addition to this work; but want of means has
alone debarred me from thus complying to the demands of
public taste.

This may, perhaps, be the most fitting and proper place
to say, that in my former work,—" The Genius of the
Peak," a small volume, consisting of a variety of short poems,
written in comparative childhood, there is much which my
now more mature judgment would gladly expunge.

The frequent use of the egotistical "I," in this production, may demand some reason or apology; but if I have not
failed in other more important matters of taste, I shall not
feel much compunction with being taunted on this head.
Should the nice critic condescend to scan a few pages of this
rather hastily written work, let him bear in mind my inap-
propriate situation in life for the attaining of philological
perfection: and the utter impossibility in my case of bestow-
ing what is so imperatively required in writing a work,
namely, almost undivided attention. A few verbal errors
(too glaring, however, to be attributed to the writer) I have
discovered here and there in this work; but when too late
for remedy.

If this, my little production, should be deemed unworthy of
notice, let it be remembered that I can truly and justly say,

> " *Me*, who never listened to the voice of praise,
> The silence of neglect can ne'er appal."—BEATTIE.

Eyam, June, 1842,   THE AUTHOR.

CONTENTS.

SUBSCRIBERS.

EYAM.

	Copies.
Andrew, Mr. Philemon ...	1
Bromley, Mr. Samuel ...	1
Beeley, Mr. John	1
Beeley, Mr. George	1
Barker, Mr. James	1
Cooper, Mr. William ...	1
Cooper, Mr. John	1
Casson, Rev. J., Curate ...	3
Cocker, Mr. Francis... ...	1
Cocker, Mr. John	1
Cocker, Mr. Edmund ...	1
Daniel, Mr. George	1
Daniel, Mr. Joseph	1
Dane, Mr. William	1
Drabble Mr. Benjamin ...	
Fentem, Mr. Thomas, Surgeon, Eyam Terrace ...	4
Furness, Mr. Samuel ...	1
Furness, Mr. Richard, Author of the "Rag-bag," "Medicus Magus," &c...	1
Froggatt, Mrs. John... ...	1
Froggatt, Mr. William, Jun.	1
Froggatt, Mr. Christopher	1
Gregory, Mr. Thomas, Solicitor	1
Gregory, Mr. William ...	1
Gregory, Miss	1
Gibson, Mr. John	1
Hall, Mr. William	1
Hill, Mr. Francis	1

	Copies.
Oaks, Mr. Edward	1
Platt, George, Esq.	2
Pursglove, Miss Elizabeth	1
Redfearn, Mr. Nicholas ...	1
Slinn, Mr. John	1
Slinn, Mr. James	1
Slinn, Mr. Robert	1
Slinn, Mr. Samuel	1
Siddall, Mr. Verdan... ...	1
Turner, Mr. Samuel ...	1
Unwin, Mr. Isaac	1
Wright, John, Esq., Firs...	2
Wright Peter, Esq., Eyam Hall...	2
Wood, Miss Jane	1
Walker, Mr. Thomas ...	1

STONEY MIDDLETON.

	Copies.
Buxton, Mr. George ...	1
Cocker, Mr. Edmund ...	1
Denman, Lord Chief Justice	1
Furness, Mr. Peter	1
Furness, Mr. Thomas ...	1
Higginbotham, Mr. Robert	1
Hallam, Mr. William ...	1
Lancake, Mr. John	1
Lancake, Miss Martha ...	1

GRINLDEFORD BRIDGE.

	Copies.
Andrew, Mr. Joseph ...	1

Outram, Mr. Robert... ... 2

HATHERSAGE.

Child, Mr. Tobias 1
Cocker, Mr. Henry 1
Darvil, Mr. J. 1
Frith, Mr. Micah (Lead Mill) 1
Greaves, Mr. 1
Marsden, Mr. Thomas ... 1
Martin, Mr. William ... 1
Ross, Rev. —— 1
Sherriff, Mr. —— 1
Smith, Mr. —— 1
Wiggitt, Mr. —— 1

BRETTON & FOOLOW.

Mortin, Mr. Anthony ... 1
Mortin, Mr. Joseph 1
Middleton, Mr. John ... 1

CRESSBROOK.

Heathcote, Mr. Richard ... 1
Ross, Mr. Alexander ... 1
Tymm, Mr., Monsaldale... 1

LONGSTONE.

Furness, Mr. Matthew ... 1
Furness, Miss 1
Longson, James, Esq. ... 1
Scott, Mr. Joseph 1

CALVER.

Bromeley, Mr. William ... 1
Broomhead, Mr. Thomas... 1
Clark, Mr. John 1
Highgate, ——, Esq. 1
M—— Mr.... 1

BASLOW AND CHATS-WORTH.

Archwell, Mr. Richard ... 1

Broomhead, Mr. J., Cock-hill 1
Bailey, Mr. —— 1
Frost, Mr. Matthew 1
Ludgate, Mr. Robert ... 1
Marples, Mr. John 1
Marples, Mr. Joseph ... 1
Paxton, Mrs. —— 1
Steward, Mr. Alexander ... 1
Thornhill, Mr. J. 1
White, Mr. John 1

BAKEWELL AND ASH-FORD.

Barker, G. R., Esq.... ... 1
Cavendish, Hon. G. H., M.P. 1
Cowe, Mr. George 1
Coke, D'Ewes, Esq. ... 4
Goodwin, Mr. J., Stationer 3
Greaves, Mr. John 1
Price, Mr. 1
Gratten, Mr. 1
Harrison, Mr. 1
Hully, Mr. 1
Mozley, Mr. George... ... 6
Rooke, Rev, T. J. 1
Sellars, Mr. Benjamin ... 1
Underwood, Captain ... 1

HASSOP AND BEELEY.

His Lordship the Earl of Newburgh 2
Wainwright, Mr. 1
Holms, Mr. J. 1
Martin, Mr. 1
Travers, Mr. J., Cauton... 1

HYDE, GLOSSOP, AND MOTTRAM.

Buckley, Mr. James... ... 1
Bradshaw, Mr. Samuel ... 1
Furness, Mr. Peter 1
Lawton, Mr. John 1
Ridgeway, Mr. Isaac ... 1

	Copies.
Blinn, Mr. James	1
Taylor, Mr. Samuel... ...	1
Wagstaff, Mr. John	1

MACCLESFIELD.

	Copies.
Bennet, Mr. Edward ...	1
Chaloner, Mr. George ...	1
Draper, Mr. William ...	1
Dewhurst, Mr. J.	1
Godier, Mr. George... ...	1
Royse, Mr. Isaac	1
Unwin, Mr. Robert	1
Willson, Mr. Richard ...	1

SHEFFIELD.

	Copies.
Ward, S. B., Esq., Mount Pleasant	1
Bramwell, Mr. Robert ...	1
Broomhead, Mr. John ...	1
Brittlebank, Mr. Joseph ...	1
Booth, Mr. John	1
Bardwell, Mr. T. N., jun...	1
Bridgeford, Mr. John ...	1
Cocking, Mr.	1
Elliott, Mr. E., Author of the "Corn Law Rhymes," &c.	1
Eyre, Mr. Samuel	1
Fisher, Mr. F.	1
Fisher, Mr. C.	1
Favell, Mr. W. F., surgeon	1
Fisher, Mr. R.	1
Frith, Mr. J.	1
Fowler, Mr. John	1
Gilbee, Mr.	1
Horncastle, Mr Henry ...	1
Hinde, Mr. Charles	1
Hall, Mr. Spencer T., the Sherwood Forester ...	1
Hobson, Mr. John	1
M., Rev. J., and Friend ...	3
Newbould, Mr. William ...	1
Oldfield, Mr. William ...	1
Oglesby, Mr. James... ...	1
Pindar, Mr.	1

	Copies.
Roberts, Samuel, Esq. ...	1
Rodgers, Mr. Henry... ...	1
Ryalls, Mr. John	1
Ramsay, Mr. Richard ...	1
Staniforth, Mr. J.	1
Stevenson, Mr. J.	1
Waterfall, Mr. H.	1
Warburton, Mr, William...	1
Willis, Miss Sarah	1
Whitaker, Mr. A.	1
Wood, Miss Elizabeth ...	1
Wood, Mr. Joseph F. ...	7

MANCHESTER.

	Copies.
Blomeley, Mr. James ...	1
Blomeley, Mr. John... ...	1
Burgess, Mr. William ...	1
Butterworth, Mr. James ...	1
Furness, Mr. Matthew ...	1
Fox, Mr. Richard	1
Fielding, Mr., Salford ...	1
Jackson, Mr.	1
Lowe, Mr. John	1
Lowe, Mr. William	1
Lowe, Mr. James	1
Kershaw, Mr. Jonathan ..	1
Kershaw, Mr. John	1
Kershaw, Mr. William ...	1
Roberts, Mr.	1
Shannon, Mr.	1
White, Mr. Isaac	1
Willson, Mr. George ...	1

MISCELLANEOUS PLACES.

	Copies.
Atkinson, Mr. J., Chesterfield	1
Bradshaw, Mr. Joseph, Brampton	1
Bradley, Captain, Brincliffe	1
Bramwell, Mr. W. Chapel-en-le-Frith	1
Bardsley, Mr.. Do. ...	1
Brownsword, Mr., Stockport	1
Elletson, D. H., Park Hall, Lancashire	1

Copies.		Copies.
Evans, W., Esq., M.P., Allestre	7	Newton, W., Esq., Tideswell	3
Fox, Mr., Chapel-en-le-Frith	1	Proctor, Gilbert, Camforth Lodge, Lancashire	1
Fentem, Miss Ann, Tickhill	1	Pearson, Mr. J. T., Comisbro'	1
Gisbourne, Thomas, Esq., Horwich House	4	Shenton, Rev. R., Hucklow	12
Holt, John, Esq., Rusholme Lodge, near Manchester.	2	Swallow, Mr., Holmfirth	1
		Swinscoe, Mr. T., Buxton.	1
Lee, Thomas, Ashover	1	Teasdale, Mr., Youlgreave.	1
McKay, Mr. Robert, bookseller, Matlock	6	Tomlin, Mr. R., Knowchley	1
		Wain, Mr. John, Axedge	1
Mitchell, Mr., Flagg	1	Walker, Mr., Matlock	1
Middleton, M. M., Esq., Leam Hall	1	Wood, Mr. F., Liverpool	4

ERRATA.

PAGE 20th—4th line from bottom, for *battled* read *brattled*.
— 40th—13th   do.   for *proscribed* read *prescribed*.
— 44th—15th   do.   for *affected* read *infected*.
— 52d—9th   do.   do.   do.
— 67th—17th line from top for *cut* read *rock*.
— 69th—16th   do.   for *convalescency* read *to convalescence*.
— 81st—16th   do.   for *Mompesson's* read *Mompesson*.
— 124th—5th   do.   for *Sepulchre* read *Sepulture*.

THE

HISTORY AND ANTIQUITIES

OF

EYAM.

"Around the precincts of my tranquil home,
I *know* each barren spot, each cultured nook."
J. C. PRINCE.

"Lovely village! afar thy name is spread
Throughout this land.   Alas! 'tis not alone
By rural charms that pilgrims here are led :—
They come to gaze upon each field-gravestone
That tells what thou lone village once hast known :—
When pestilence with direful, black'ning breath,
With a dread fury raged till then unknown,
And sudden swept, as each memorial saith,
The trembling village throng into the arms of death."
W. W.

THE village of Eyam has been long characterized
throughout the Peak of Derbyshire, as the birth-
place of genius—the seat of the Muses—the
Athens of the Peak, and the like.   That it is
justly entitled to these classical encomiums, I shall
not presume to affirm.   Certain it is, however,
that the once renowned Nightbroder, Miss Anna

B

Seward, Richard Furniss, and other inferior
minstrels were born at Eyam; and equally certain
it is, that while residing at Eyam the highly-gifted,
but unfortunate Cunningham, tuned his harmo-
nious, sylvan shell, and sang his happiest lays.
But hallowed as is this romantic village by giving
birth and residence to these celebrated characters,
it has, however, another and a stronger claim to
general notice—the terrible PLAGUE by which it
was so singularly visited, and almost wholly de-
populated, in the years A.D. 1665 and 1666: the
details of which calamity must, however, necessarily follow a brief description of the location,
scenery, antiquities, and Manor, of this highly interesting village.

Eyam is a village and parish in the North or
High Peak of Derbyshire. It is comprised in the
Hundred of the High Peak,—in the Honours of
Peveril and Tutbury;—and in the ecclesiastical
jurisdiction of the Archdeaconry of Derby, and in
the Diocese of Lichfield and Coventry. The
village stands in the south-east part of the parish,
six miles north of Bakewell, and nearly in the
centre of a line drawn from Sheffield to Buxton :
being twelve miles distant from each place. It
contains about 180 houses, and according to the
census of 1841, 954 inhabitants; who are chiefly
employed in agriculture, lead mining, and cotton
and silk weaving. The parish is nearly circular,
about four miles in diameter, and includes the
hamlets of Foolow and Eyam Woodlands. It
abuts on the parishes of Hope, Hathersage, and
Bakewell; and the following places and streams
mark its boundary:—a rivulet near to Stoney Middleton Church-yard—top of Stoke-wood—Goat-
cliffe brook—the river Derwent—Highlow brook

—top of Grindlow—Wardlow Miers—Foundley-
fence—and the Dale Brook to where it receives the
rivulet first mentioned. Small as is this parish,
yet it contained an uncommon tract of moorland
until the year A.D. 1801, when an Act was obtained for its inclosure : a circumstance which has,
by the bulk of the parishioners, been greatly regretted. The village forms a long street, nearly
a mile in length, built apparently, as it is approached from Middleton Dale, on a ledge or
table-land of limestone. The stratum of this
stone seems wholly composed of marine exuviæ,
abounding with a variety of shells: entronchi,
coralloids, madrapores, and many other species of
crustaceous animals. In this stratum of limestone
the greatest caverns abound :—in fact, Eyam is
built on a series of caverns, many of which have
been explored to a great extent—chiefly for the
beautiful and fanciful stalactites with which they
are so richly adorned. The village runs from east
to west in a serpentine form ; and, as Gilbert
White has observed of Selbourne, the cartway
divides two most incongruous soils. The houses,
in most places, on the north side, stand just where
the grit or sandstone stratum commences; whilst
those on the south side are built invariably on the
limestone; and though the village is so very long,
the same diversification occurs throughout.

The several parts of the village are thus named :
—the Townend, which is the eastern part, and
from which branch the Lydgate, the Water-lane,
the Dale, the Cocy or Causeway,—the Cross, or
middle of the village,—the Townhead, or the extreme western part. Contiguous to the street,
and nearly in the centre of the village, stands the
Church, a very ancient fabric, which from its being

encircled by large umbrageous trees, has often
excited the notice and admiration of strangers.

Of the origin and signification of the name of
this old English village—Eyam—there is but little
that is satisfactory known. That this was not the
original name of the village is very probable
indeed: in fact, there is some mention in some
very old work, that its name before the Norman
Conquest was *Mosse*, and that in consequence of a
battle, fought on the heights a little north of Eyam,
the name of the village was changed to something
like its present name, in honour of the victorious
chief. That there is any good foundation for this
matter I cannot say; having, after a very tedious
search, been unable to meet with the account. Of
the validity of this story the following circumstances
may be considered as evidence :—all that plot of
land behind the Church at Eyam, known as the
Nar, or more properly, *Near Crofts*, was once a
fenny bog, covered very deeply with moss, which
circumstance *might* give the name of *Mosse* to
the adjoining habitations; and that a battle was
fought on Eyam-moor, in some past age, there is
abundant proof in the warlike weapons found there
at various times; and also in the very current tradition of that event. It is very singular that this
certainly ancient village is not mentioned in the
Norman survey by any thing like its present name;
and that such is the case, there is every reason to
believe; while there is a strong probability that it
had a priest and a church long anterior to that
period. Stoney Middleton, a village very near
Eyam, and of smaller extent, is noticed in the
survey of Edward the Confessor, yet its name—
Middleton—gives prior existence to Eyam. To
notice all the conjectures concerning the intrinsic

meaning of the name—Eyam—would be tiresome
even to the etymologist; a few, however, of the
most plausible will not, it is hoped, be deemed in-
trusive and insignificant.

Some imagine that the original meaning of
the word has been lost through its having been
written so variously at different times. In the
reign of Henry the Sixth it was written *Eyham*—
in fact, it has had all the following modes of spelling :—*Wyham, Eam, Eyme, Hame, Eme, Hyme,
Eyham*, and *Eyam :* the last form only is now
generally recognized. A little north of Eyam,
there is a small place called *Bretton,* which name
is very ancient, and means *mountainous.* The
word is pure Celtic, and it was the name of England long before the Roman invasion. This little
place, being in the parish of Eyam, and having
retained a name of such high antiquity has induced
some few to suppose that the word—Eyam—in
some of its forms of spelling, may be of the same
ancient source; of which word, however, the
meaning appears to be (according to this supposition) irrecoverably lost.* One of the two following conjectures, comes most probably the
nearest to the true signification.

In the word *Eyam,* we have undoubtedly the
ham, or *am,* the common Saxon termination ex-
pressive of residence; but of what the *Ey* is sig-
nificant, is not so manifest. One of the conjectures alluded to, states that the *Ey* is a corruption

* Creighton, in his Introduction to his Dictionary of Scripture
Names, observes that Dr. Johnson and other modern lexico-
graphers, have greatly erred in seeking (and pretending to find)
the origin of western tongues in Greek and Latin. He further
states, that a knowledge of the Celtic is indispensable in tracing
the true origin of the names of places, rivers, and monuments in
the West of Europe.

of the adjective *High ;* and that the original signification of the compound word *Eyam,* was *High-
dwelling, High-place,* or *High-hamlet :* this, considering the locality of the village, its proximity to
Sir William, one of the highest mountains in the
Peak, is far from being improbable.* The other
conjecture derives the *Ey,* from *Ea,* water, which,
with the residential *ham,* or *am,* means a residence
amidst, or by a superfluity of water. The great
quantity of water with which Eyam must always
have been supplied, renders this supposition more
than probable. In the centre of the village there
is a pool vulgarly called the river, which name is a
corruption of *Eaver,* or *Ever-water :* an appellation properly descriptive of this pool, which with
the numberless springs and rivulets in and around
the village, give a strong probability that the word
—Eyam—may signify the *Water-place,* or *The
Village of Waters.*† According to tradition, and
other evidences, the village once stood in what is
called Eyam-edge ; and this is strongly countenanced by the fact, that where the greater part of
the village now stands, was once covered with the
works of lead mines ; and to such an extent, that
it is very common for old openings, or shafts, to
fall in under the thresholds, pantries, and floors of
the houses, and under the street and other places
where none was known to the inhabitants to exist.
In the Edge, traces of the foundations of habitations have frequently been discovered. This circumstance has been mentioned as a probable cause
for some change in the name of the village. In
fine, it may be observed of this vague and unsatisfactory subject, that whatever may be the signifi-

* Vide, Genius of the Peak, page 116.
† Vide, Medicus Magus, page 58.

cation of the name of the village; that whether it
has changed its name or not; it has now a name
which the poet wished that to be of an old English
village which he met with, namely: "no common
name":—

> " Thy name I know not nor would know,—
> No common name would I be told;
> Yet often shall I seek thee now,—
> Thou village quaint and old."—R. HOWITT.

The scenery of Eyam has but few parallels: it
is highly varied and picturesque. In the eastern
part of the village the cottages are generally man-
tled with ivy, adorned with fruit trees, and shaded
by wide-spreading sycamores. In some parts the
cottages are grotesquely clustered together; in
other parts they stand apart, flanked with bee-
hives, and with their eaves of straw bestudded with
nests of the household sparrow; altogether forming
a scene, delightful as rare. This rural and highly
romantic picture is greatly heightened by the grey
tower of the Church, which picturesquely overtops
this part of the village, rising from the centre of a
beautiful circle of linden trees, which encompass the
Church-yard like giant sentinels, guarding the
sacred precincts of the silent dead. Amidst these
homely cottages there are some mansions of excellent structure, which for elegance and number far
excel those of any other village in Derbyshire.

Northward of the village, a mountain range,
nearly 600 feet high, runs parallel with the village,
crowned with plantations of rising trees. This
lofty range is to the village an impenetrable screen,
to ward off the biting, boreal blasts: the village
lying, as it were, beneath its sheltering height, in
peaceful, calm repose. How beautiful the pros-

pect from this lofty eminence.   Thence the eye
may behold—

" —— ancient hamlets nestling far below,
And many a wild wood walk, where childhood's footsteps go."
                                        J. C. PRINCE.

A little farther north, nearly in the centre of the
parish, rises Sir William—the Parnassus of the
Peak ; a mountain of great altitude, and honoured
by numberless classical associations. From the
summit of this Prince of Derbyshire hills, the eye
extends over countless hills and luxuriant dales.
Masson, Ax-edge, Mam Tor, Kinderscout, and
Stanage lift up their hoary heads and, beckoning
to Sir William, tell in language stronger than
words, of a companionship of ages. How rapturous
must be the feelings of the tourist who mounts the
peak of this mountain, and with fire-kindled eye
beholds on every hand the uneffaced handmarks of
Nature! How joyous his sensations to perceive
in such goodly profusion, the perceptible and
original traces of the finger of God! Beautiful
mountain! ever shall I remember standing on thy
summit at the decline of a hot summer's day ; the
sinking sun tinged with gold the peaks of far distant hills, which shone severally in the distance
like well remembered joys in the memory of the
past. But anon, this lovely scene was changed :
I beheld the clouds, old couriers of the sky, mar-
shalling the elements to war; the distant mountains
put on their misty robes, as if conscious of the im-
pending storm. Soon I saw the vivid lightning
flash ; the thunder battled in the rear; and in the
midst of this sublime scene I almost unconsciously
repeated the following exquisite lines of Byron,
changing without premeditation the words " Jura,"

and "joyous Alps," to "Mam Tor," and "Sir William high"—

"————————— Far along
From peak to peak, the rattling crags among
Leaps the live thunder! Not from one lone cloud,
But every mountain now hath found a tongue,
And *Mam Tor* answers, through her misty shroud,
Back to *Sir William* high, who calls to her aloud."

Drenched with rain, I gazed with profound emotion on the elemental strife; and in the calm which ensued I heard "the small still voice," with the awe and reverence of the Patriarch of old.

"—— God curbs the lightning, stills the roar,
And earth smiles through her tears more lovely than before."

                                                J. C. PRINCE.

A little to the east of Eyam is Riley, or the Hill of Graves—a noble and pleasing feature in the romantic character of the village. Rising on high, with its steepy, wood-clad slope, it gives to the village a richly picturesque appearance. The varied and indescribable scenery in this direction is bounded on one hand by the sable rocks of Corbor, and the singularly built village of Stoney Middleton, a great part of which forms a portion of the parish of Eyam.

On the south side of the village two dells branch parallel with each other into Middleton Dale. One, provincially called the Delf, or Delve, is a most secluded and beautiful place. It has all the natural beauty and seclusion of the valley of Rasselas. Hanging tors, pensile cliffs, Cucklet church, shadowy trees, blooming flowers, a winding rill, tuneful birds, are only a few of the rural charms of this incomparable dell. At the western extremity of this lonely retreat is an extensive chasm, or cleft, known by the undignified appellation,—Salt Pan; it extends throughout the whole mass of limestone rock, and the projections on the one side, and indentations on the other, fully indicate that this vast mass of rock was rent asunder by some mighty convulsion of nature in some distant age of the world. A small stream issues from the mouth of the chasm, and winds its way amongst beds of moss, fern, and flowers. Often have I sat musing over the purling stream in the chasm, until I fancied myself in the Egerian Grotto. Ah!

    " This cave was surely shaped out for the greeting
      Of an enamoured Goddess, and the cell
   Haunted by holy love—the earliest oracle."— BYRON.

The other dell, known as Eyam Dale, is rich in rural scenery. On one side it is bounded by grey towering rocks, crested with ivy and other foliage. Some few of these rocks, however, are naked, exhibiting a sort of grimness that forms a pleasing contrast. The other side of this dell is covered with rising wood, amongst which there are numerous winding paths, that lead to a place called "the Rock Garden," where for ages the lovers of Eyam have breathed " the tender tale." A dancing rill winds through the dell, murmuring most musically to the lonely ear. This dell, and in fact the whole village, may be said to be another Anathoth—a place of responses, or echoes. In several approximate places a clear pollysyllabical echo exists. Such is a portion of the very imperfectly described scenery of this secluded village; which has frequently been noticed to be the best specimen of an old English village now to be met with.

Throughout the whole of this parish are scattered many elegant and substantial dwellings— some for situation and elegance are rarely to be met with at so great a distance from places of commerce. Amongst the latter description is

Leam Hall, the residence of M. M. Middleton,
Esq., an old English gentleman, alike distinguished
for urbanity, good sense, and literary taste.* This
singularly neat villa stands in the midst of ornamented grounds ; and when contrasted with the
mountain scenery in the circling distance, it has
all the charms of an oasis in a desert. The exterior decorations of this rural seat have often excited
the admiration of tourists. Stoke Hall, a little out
of the parish, is another of this class of buildings.
Still nearer the verge of the parish, in Stoney Middleton, is the much admired country seat of Lord
Chief Justice Denman, — whose richly entitled
fame as a lawyer and judge ; and whose poetical
taste, as evinced in his translation of the famous
song on Harmodius and Aristogiton,† render this
place of his occasional residence greatly attractive.
Many other well-built habitations may be seen in
all places throughout the parish — in Foolow,
Hazleford, Stoney Middleton, and Grindleford
Bridge ; besides solitary farm houses on the hills
and in the valleys of this locality, which is justly
characterised in the following language of the
poet :—

> " A realm of mountain, forest-haunt, and fell,
> And fertile valleys, beautifully lone ;
> Where fresh and far romantic waters roam,
> Singing a song of peace by many a cottage home."
>
> J. C. PRINCE.

The varied and romantic scenery of this place,
as may be expected, has distinguished the inhabitants by a character peculiarly antique. Before
the present century the villagers of Eyam exhibited
all the characteristics so observable in the inhabi-

---

* M. M. Middleton, Esq. is the author of a work entitled
" Poetical Sketches of a Tour,"—written for private circulation.
        † Vide Bland's Anthology.

tants of mountainous districts.   Even now a notion
prevails of keeping themselves distinct by inter-
marriages.   They are exceedingly tenacious of the
preservation of their genealogies,—a consequence
of having dwelt in one place for successive generations.   Hence their observance of customs from
time immemorial; hence their adherence to here-
ditary prejudices; hence their numerous legends,
handed down from time immemorial; and hence
that unity of interest for which they have been so
singularly distinguished in times past.   It is lamentable, however, that the physical condition of
the present inhabitants of this far-famed village is
greatly inferior to that of their forefathers: the
principal cause of which is the decay of the lead
mines.   Previously to the present century, each
miner had his cow and small plot of land, to which
he attended during the intervals of his work at the
mine; this double employment yielded him sufficient to live in health and happiness, leaving him
abundance of time for halesome recreation.   The
mines being under water, can no longer in their
present condition be successfully worked: and this
deplorable circumstance is fast changing the aspect
and character of the village.   It, however, still
retains a few of the endearing marks of the old
English village: a few old pastimes fondly kept; a
smattering of happy harvest scenes; and the holy
welcome of the Sabbath morn.   These still remain
to call up a thousand recollections of once happier
times: when sweet content and plenty dwelled
within the rustic cot.

The ANTIQUITIES of Eyam are not very numerous, but interesting.   Those of nature are remarkable.   About twenty years ago, Mr. Anthony
Hancock, of Foolow, found in a limestone quarry,

near Eyam, a petrified snake coiled up in a ring, very perfect. It went into the collection of some eminent antiquarian, where it will, probably, be treasured as a very singular curiosity. Of this once living animal, it may be observed, that, while the mortal part of hundreds of generations has returned to its pristine elements, this reptile has retained its identical form through the lapse of un-numbered ages. A little more than thirty years ago, Mr. James Wood, Eyam, was engaged in cutting a large sandstone on Eyam-moor, when, to his utter surprise and astonishment, he found im-bedded in the stone a petrified fish about a foot in length. It was perfect in every part—gill and tail. This phenomenon tends to disturb some geological theories.

But it is the Druidical remains, a little north of Eyam, which excite the liveliest interest in anti-quarians; which remains prove, to a certain degree, the high antiquity of Eyam. All that tract of land called Eyam-moor, was, until its inclosure, literally covered with these relics of ante-historic times. The Druidical temple, or circle, on that part of the moor called Wet-withins, is frequently visited. It consists of sixteen oblong sandstones, standing in an upright position, forming a circle about thirty yards in diameter. The stones are nearly equal in size, standing about a yard high, except on the north side, where two or three are enveloped in heath, and therefore appear, though clearly visible, not so large as the others. This circle is still fur-ther distinguished by a circular mound of earth, about three feet high, in which the stones are placed. In the centre, there stood, until some years back, a large stone, which was, undoubtedly, the altar on which human sacrifices were made.

c

It was also the *Maen Gorsedd* (or stone of Assembly.) The ceremony used at the opening of the *Gorseddau* (or meetings) was the sheathing of the sword on the *Maen Gersedd*, at which all the Druid priests assisted. All the places of meeting were, like this, set apart by forming a circle of earth and stones around the *Maen Gorsedd*. This circle was called *Cylch Cyngrair*, or circle of Federation; and the priest, or bard, who recited the traditions and poems, was named the *Dudgeiniad*, or the Reciter. The *Dudgeiniad*, dressed in a uni-coloured robe, always commenced his recitations by one of the following mottos :— " In the eye of the light, and in the face of the sun ;"—" The truth against the world." It is singular that this circle has not been more noticed, seeing that it is far more perfect than many, more particularly described.

How deeply impressed with sensations of veneration must be the contemplative mind, when he stands within this circle, which has been, some thousands of years ago, the theatre on which the ancient Briton displayed his knowledge, patriotism, and eloquence. This veneration, however, is diminished when we reflect on some of the bloody and unholy sacrifices said to have been made by the Druids.

Let us for a few moments fly back on the wings of thought, through the dim vista of two thousand years; let us imagine ourselves standing near this very spot, looking at the mysterious and bloody rites of the Druids. Behold within this very circle a lovely female is laid upon the central bloody stone ; trembling with horror at the awful scene around her. About the place a countless throng look on with profound emotion, watching the victim with anxious solicitude. The fire on the altar burns dimly; noisy and discordant music incessantly plays to drown the victim's cries. All is now hushed, and the white-robed priest, with an infernal joy, approaches his shivering victim, brandishing his knife; and oh! horrible! plunges it into her heaving bosom; and in an instant tears out her reeking heart and casts it into the fire. Terrific scene! Let us return to this our day, and rejoice in the utter abolishment of the sacrifice of human beings.

In the immediate vicinity of this circle there are at least twelve more, each surrounded with circular mounds of earth, and some with stones. Most of these, as they are not above twelve yards in diameter, must be sepulchral; this is evident, for there appears to have been in all of them, a large heap of stones in the centre; under which stones, urns have been buried, but are now taken away.*

Contiguous to the large circle, or temple, there was, until some years back, one of the most interesting barrows in the Peak of Derbyshire. It covered an area of ground from twenty-five to thirty yards in diameter. It was in the form of a cone, ten or twelve yards high, when perfect; and was composed wholly of small stones. On opening this cairn, or barrow, a many years ago, an unbaked urn was found containing ashes, bones, an arrow-head of flint, and a little charcoal with which the body had been burned. The person interred in this cairn was certainly some great chief or king; for according to some authors, it was the custom of the aboriginals of this Island, to express their abhorrence of a tyrant or other wicked person

* Vide Brown, on Urn Burial.

after death, by casting a stone at the place of his
sepulture as often as they passed it; and thus were
accumulated the large piles of stones, under which
urns, containing ashes and bones, have been found.
In the Highlands of Scotland, it is common to this
day, to say contemptuously, " I shall cast a stone
at thy grave some day." There is, in the neighbourhood of Eyam, a very popular tradition of
some great chief, or king, having been buried in
this barrow; and it has been frequently explored
in search of something appertaining to him.
Nothing, however, has ever been found except the
urn; but in the vicinity, spears, arrow-heads, axes,
hatchets, and a many other remains of antiquity
have been turned up.   About a mile west of this
barrow there was, about forty years ago, another
of great dimensions: it stood on Hawley's piece.
The diameter at the base was twenty-two yards,
and about twelve yards high.   When the Moor
was enclosed, it was carried away to make fences.
An urn of great size was found near the centre on
the ground, and was carried away to the residence
of the person who found it; but was afterwards
broken and buried.*   Another barrow unexplored
may be seen in Eyam-edge, near the Old Twelve-
meer's mine.   It is about forty yards in diameter
at the base, and about eight or ten yards high.   In
the top there is a dimple or cavity, which, according to Pilkington, is a manifest proof that it is
British.   Dr. Borlace, however, thinks that such
are Roman; but in this, I imagine, he is mistaken.

* The person who had this precious relic of antiquity, was
persuaded by his silly neighbours, that it was unlucky to have
such a thing in his house; and on losing a young cow, he immediately buried it.

Indeed the whole parish north of the village, is even now bestudded with barrows, cairns, mounds, and other remains of antiquity.

One large stone on the Moor has been a great object of curiosity, from its having a circular cavity in the top about a foot in diameter, and the same in depth. The stone is of an extraordinary size—by far the largest on the Moor. It is conjectured to have been the altar, or central stone of some large circle, but of which there is no trace now. That this place was one of the principal places of the Druids there are numberless proofs; but as it is out of the road to any place of note, it has been rarely noticed.

Numberless urns have been found at various times around Eyam. About forty years ago, in making the road called the Occupation Road, a beautiful urn, richly decorated, was found by Mr. S. Furness, Eyam; it contained nothing but ashes. Around the place where the urn was found, the earth appeared to have been burnt, which circumstance, according to Wormius, would lead us to believe it to be Danish. This author states, in his funeral ceremonies of the Danes, that " The deceased was brought out into the fields, where they made an oblong place with great stones, and there burned the body, and then collected the ashes into an urn, round which they set great stones; casting up over it a mound of earth and stones." Respectable as is this authority, it is nevertheless doubtful, as will be seen from the following contents of an urn found within a few yards of this.

Not many years ago, two men, Joseph Slinn and William Redfearn, were working near the Bole-hill, Eyam, when they discovered an urn surrounded with stones. Slinn wishing to procure it

entire, went to a distance for a spade; in the
meanwhile, Redfearn, thinking it might contain
some treasure, immediately dashed it to pieces,
when, to his utter mortification, he found it contained only some ashes and two copper coins. One
of the coins was lost on the spot, but was found
some years after, when I saw it, and found it to
contain the inscription, *Maximianus*, and something else not legible: probably Dioclesian, as
Maximianus and Dioclesian were joint Emperors of
the Roman Empire.* As these two urns were
very similar, and buried so near together, it is highly
probable that they were Roman; at least, containing Roman coin implies as much. Another
urn was found in the Mag-clough, Eyam,—a very
large one: this was buried again afterwards.
Robert Broomhead, Eyam, broke one to pieces in
taking the foundation of an old wall up, at Riley,
about fourteen years ago. One was found forty
years since in Riley-side, in which was some
ancient weapons and arrow-heads of flint. Two
cairns or borrows were destroyed on the top of
Riley, a many years since, in which were found
urns containing ashes and bones. There is also
some recollection of a very large circle of stones,
or very high, unhewn pillars, near to those barrows,
which stones were surrounded by a circular mound
of earth. The circle had an entrance, if not two,
something like that mentioned by Dr. Stukeley, at

* Maximianus (M. Arul. Valer. Hercul.) born in Sirmium.
He entered early into the Roman army, and exhibited so much
valour, that the Emperor Dioclesian, in A.D. 286, shared the
Empire with him. The cruelty of Maximianus towards the
Christians is almost incredible. During his short career 144,000
were put to death, and 700,000 banished. He quitted the Empire with Dioclesian, and hanged himself at Marseilles in A.D.,
310.—BAYLE.

Abury, North Wiltshire. This celebrated antiquarian makes the Druidical remains at Abury,
to have been in a form, symbolical of the serpent;
and it is matter of regret, that he had not his attention directed to the numerous druidical remains
at Eyam, for in his time they were certainly more
perfect.* As, from what is already shewn, the
Druids abounded so greatly, and had numberless
temples around Eyam, it is natural to suppose that
there would be some traces of their customs still
observed. That such is the case there is ample
evidence.

One of the incantations practised at the festival
of the Druids was to anoint the forehead of a sick
person with May-dew, which was carefully gathered
at day-break, and the cure of course immediately
followed. Now at Eyam and its vicinity it has
been a general, and still prevailing custom to anoint
weak and deceased children with May-dew. Another part of the ceremony of the great festival of
the Druids, consisted in carrying long poles of
mountain ash festooned with flowers. Hanging
out bunches of flowers from cottage windows, so
very prevalent at Eyam on May-day, has its origin
in this Druidical ceremony. In fact, to notice all
the customs of similar origin, and still observed at
Eyam, would be tedious :—Passing the bottle or
glass, (*deas soil,*) or according to the course of
the sun; diving for apples in vessels of water;
making love-cakes, or speechless cakes; carrying
garlands before the corpses of unmarried persons;
giving cakes and singing at funerals, and numerous
other observances, have a purely Druidical origin.

* Some persons imagine to have seen the remains of a large
funeral pyre, near the Shaw-engine, Eyam-edge. To this I
cannot speak.

Gebelin and Brande have both noticed a peculiar custom practiced in Cornwall, and particularly at Penzance, the origin of which they say is lost in antiquity. The same custom is known and practiced at Eyam, in the very common plays—Loosing-tines and Long-duck. In reading an account of the antiquities of Cornwall, I was particularly struck with the identity of the two customs. The Golf, or Golfing, is said to be an amusement peculiar to the Highlands of Scotland, where it has been practiced from time immemorial. The same diversion is known at Eyam, by the uncouth name—*Seg.* Goose-riding, about half a century since, was at Eyam a very common, but barbarous amusement. The hopper-baulk; bees knitting on a dead branch, are considered to be certain prognostications of death. The Druidical customs and other observances may be deemed trifling and unimportant; but there was something of weight connected with the origin of each; at least they prove, to some degree, the great antiquity of the place where they are still observed.

That Eyam is a very ancient place may be still further ascertained. The word "Tor" is said to be of Phœnician origin, and this word is very common at Eyam:—The Tor Tops, the Shining Tor, the Hanging Tor, are all in its immediate vicinity. Bole, a word equally common, signified anciently the hearth on which the lead was melted: the boles were made on the western brows of Tors. Bole is an eastern word, which means a lump of metal. These, with numerous other words, can be clearly traced to an Asiatic source, which is a demonstrative proof that the mines in and around Eyam, were worked anciently either by a colony of foreigners, or under their direction. We are

certain that the mines of the Peak were worked in
very early times; some think before the Roman
invasion; certainly, however, by the Romans, or
their enslaved Britons. It is unnecessary to refer
to the several pieces of lead found near Matlock,
bearing the inscriptions of Roman Emperors. On
Eyam-moor, small pieces of lead have been found
in every direction : one weighing fourteen pounds
was met with beneath the surface very lately; and
about thirty years since, in planting some ground
near to Leam Hall, belonging to M. M. Middleton, Esq., a conical piece of lead was found, weighing between thirty and forty pounds. It was a
yard in length, and had a hook or handle attached
to it, whereby it had been disengaged from the
mould in which it was cast.

That the Romans had, at least, a temporary residence in or around Eyam, we have satisfactory
evidence in the finding of Roman coins and other
articles. In the year A.D. 1814, some persons
employed in bareing limestone in Eyam Dale, found
a great quantity of Roman coins, some silver and
some copper, bearing the inscriptions of Probus,
Gallienus, Victorinus,—Roman Emperors. These
coins were in the possession of T. Birds, Esq.,
Eyam, a highly celebrated antiquarian. About
sixty years ago, a copper coin was found on Eyam-
moor, bearing the inscription of Probus ; and near
twenty years since, a Roman copper coin was
found in the Dale, Eyam, with the inscription on
one side, Divo Claudius, or God Claudius ; on the
obverse, Consecratia, or Consecration with the
Eagle ; it is now in the possession of Mr. J. Slinn,
Eyam. In that part of Stoney Middleton, in Eyam
parish, there have been Roman coins, at various
times discovered; and a place called the Castle Hill,

bears evident traces of the mighty masters of the
world. Some spears, and various other weapons,
have been found at Ryley, Eyam, under a large
stone: they were nearly corroded away.

That the descendants of the Romans continued
to reside in and around Eyam, may be conjectured
from the language of the inhabitants. *Plaust,*
from *Plaustrum,* to plaust hay or corn, for the
eating of those articles; and *sord,* from *sordes,* the
rind of bacon, and other things. I know a many
unlettered persons who invariably use *quantum* for
quantity, and many other Latin words. There
was a word very commonly used at Eyam, some
time ago, but whence derived I am not aware.
Steven, to steven a coat: to order a coat. Rhodes
says that he has somewhere read that the Romans
erected elegant mansions among the Peak Hills.
And it is believed that the Romans continued to
reside amongst the mountains around Eyam, even
when the Saxons and Danes successively possessed
the surrounding plains. Roman remains have been
found in abundance in a many places in the neighbourhood of Eyam, Stoney Middleton, Brough,
and other villages. Indeed, it has almost been
satisfactorily proved that the sixth legion remained
in Derbyshire sometime before they marched to the
North; but there are only a few traces of the works
left, in which their taste and genius were exhibited.
Thus, then, there are some grounds for indulging
in the pleasing supposition that the place where
Eyam stands, at least, has been honoured and hallowed by the presence of the mighty conquerors of
the earth.

That the Saxons penetrated among the mountains of the Peak, and resided in and around
Eyam, numerous proofs might be adduced. Al-

most every little eminence has a Saxon name, or
termination of name :—Hay-cliffe, Shining-cliffe,
Goats-cliffe, and a very many others, too numerous
to mention. The following customs are of Saxon
origin :—

Lich is a Saxon word, signifying a dead body.
The principal gate into Eyam church-yard is to
this day called Lich-gate, or, vulgarly, Light-gate.
This is the invariable designation of the gate of the
church-yard through which the funerals pass ; and
this appellation proves, to some degree, the antiquity of the church and village. The principal
gate of Duddleston church-yard, Shropshire, is
called by the inhabitants "the Lich-gate," and
Duddleston has been particularly noticed for its
antiquity. Lich-waking, sitting with the dead
both night and day, is still practiced by the old and
wealthy families of Eyam.—The cross at Eyam is
said to be of Saxon or Danish origin. Another
once stood in Eyam-edge, and one at Cross-lowe,
Eyam ; both have been destroyed. That in the
church-yard (and of which I shall say more subsequently) once stood in that part of Eyam, called
" The Cross."

Another very ancient custom was observed at
Eyam, until within a century back. The principal
road into Eyam once, was the Lyd-gate, now
called Ligget. Lyd, or Lid, is a Saxon word, which
means to cover or protect. At this entrance into
Eyam, there was a strong gate, at which " watch
and wards were kept every night." Every effective
man who was a householder in the village, was
bound to stand in succession at this gate, from
nine o'clock at night to six in the morning, to
question any person who might appear at the gate
wishing for entrance into the village, and to give

alarm if danger were apprehended. The watch
had a large wooden halbert, or "watch-bill," for
protection, and when he came off watch in the
morning, he took the "watch-bill," and reared it
against the door of that person whose turn to
watch succeeded his; and so on in succession.
No village in England has retained and practiced
a custom so ancient, to so late a period. In the
Scriptures there are numberless allusions to this very
antique custom: as in Joshua, c. 2, v. 5, " And it
came to pass about the time of shutting the gate,"
and so on. Indeed the following distich may justly
be applied to Eyam :—

> " Here Antiquity enjoys,
> A deep and mossy sleep."—R. HOWITT.

The MANOR of Eyam is not very extensive: it
is about the same as the parish. It cannot be cor-
rectly ascertained to whom it belonged previously
to the Norman conquest; but most probably to
Elsi, a powerful and wealthy Saxon nobleman.
After the battle of Hastings it was given, along
with seven other Derbyshire Manors, and those of
Sheffield, Worksop, and a many others, to Roger
de Busli, a trusty officer to William the Conqueror.
Much of the property of De Busli, was held by
his man Roger, as feudal tenant, who was succeeded, in the reign of Henry the First, by William
de Lovetot. Matilda, the great granddaughter of
this William de Lovetot, and sole heiress of the
Lovetots, married, in the reign of Richard the First,
Gerard de Furnival: and we find that Thomas,
the son of Matilda and Gerard de Furnival, in
enumerating his manors, at the instance of the
Statute Quo Warranto, in the reign of Edward the
First, mentions himself as possessing Eyam. Joan

the heiress of the Furnivals, was married to Thomas
Nevill. The property of the Nevills passed by
marriage to the Talbots, who became on that account Barons of Furnival, afterwards Earls of
Shrewsbury. On the death of George, the sixth
Earl of Shrewsbury, Eyam became the property of
Sir George Saville, who had married Mary, his
daughter,—she was sister to the last Earl of
Shrewsbury. It remained in the Saville family
until the death of William Saville, second Marquis
of Halifax, in the year A.D. 1700; who left three
daughters, his co-heiresses, amongst whom, after
their marriage, the estates of the Savilles were
divided, by a partition deed in the sixteenth year
of George the Second. Of these three co-
heiresses, Anne married Charles Lord Bruce, son
and heir of Thomas, Earl of Ailesbury; Dorothy
married Richard, Earl of Burlington; and Mary
married Sackville, Earl of Thanet. It is generally supposed, that it was in consequence of the
very rich veins of lead ore, discovered at Eyam
about the beginning of the eighteenth century,
that these noblemen agreed to hold the Manor of
Eyam jointly, and to present a Rector to the living
(of which they had the gift) by turns.

The joint portion of the Manor belonging to
Lord Bruce, became, through marriage, or otherwise, the property of the Duke of Chandos, from
whom it passed by marriage to the Duke of Buckingham; the joint portion belonging to the Earl of
Burlington, became, through marriage, the property of the Devonshire family; and the other
joint portion has remained, up to the present, in
the family of the Earl of Thanet. Thus, the
Duke of Devonshire, the Duke of Buckingham,
and the Earl of Thanet are the present Lords of

D

the Manor of Eyam. Besides the manorial rights,
and the gift of the living, the Lords of the Manor
have little or no property in Eyam—most of the
land and other property having been sold by Sir
George Saville two centuries ago.

It may be well to notice in this place a few
popular errors connected with the Manor of Eyam,
which have crept into works of otherwise very high
merit.   Rhodes states, through misinformation,
that the Eyam estate descended from King John,
to a family of the name of Stafford, on whom it
was bestowed in consideration of certain military
services, and on the express condition, "that a
lamp should be kept perpetually burning before the
altar of St. Helen, in the parish church of Eyam."
That the Staffords of Eyam, an exceedingly ancient and wealthy family, held a great portion of
the land at Eyam on the tenure mentioned, is
probably correct; but that it emanated from the
munificence of King John, is an undoubted mistake. King John, when Earl of Montaine, had
all the confiscated estates of the Peverils granted
to him by his brother, Richard the First; but
Eyam, and other places in Derbyshire, never
formed a part of the princely possessions of the
Peverils; although Camden mentions the whole of
the county of Derby as belonging to that family.
The document containing the specification of the
grant of lands at Eyam to the Staffords, is said to
have been found at the Highlow Hall, near Eyam,
a many years since; but in whose hands it now
lies, is not publicly known. A person, however,
who saw the document at the time of its removal
from the Highlow, states, that the grant was made,
not by King John, but by some Roger: probably
Roger, the feudal tenant of De Busli, or Roger

De Busli himself. It is conjectured by some, notwithstanding the probable genuineness of the document in question, that the Staffords inherited their extensive property at Eyam, by a marriage with the Furnivals: this is countenanced by the arms of the Furnivals being, a bend between six martlets; and the Staffords, a chevron between three martlets. The Staffords were a very wealthy family, but never, as is stated in the Peak Scenery, Lords of the Manor of Eyam.

. In the reign of Richard the Second, one of the Staffords of Eyam was, for some political offence, seized in his house at Eyam, and carried away to some place of security, where he remained a close prisoner, until he was ransomed by his relatives and friends. Amongst the conservators of the peace in the county of Derby, made in the twelfth year of the reign of Henry the Sixth. A.D. 1433, we find the names of the following persons:—" John Stafford de Eyham, Richard Colyn de Eyham."* In the work referred to above, it is stated that a new mansion was erecting for the last of the Staffords who resided at Eyam, at the time of the plague, when the family left the place never to return. This is, however, a great mistake: for Humphrey, the last male of this branch of the Staffords, died at Eyam nearly a century before the plague. Of this family, their property, descendants, and habitation, more will be said subsequently. The remaining particulars of the Manor, with a few other circumstances connected with Eyam, up to the middle of the seventeenth

* This Commission was appointed to tender an oath to the Gentry, for the better observance of the peace both in themselves and retainers.—Vide Glover's History of Derbyshire, vol. 1.

century, will be found under different heads, after the following details of the terrible plague.

" THE PLAGUE
O'er hills and vales of gold and green,
Passed on, undreaded and unseen :
Foregoing cities, towns, and crowds ;
Gay mansions glittering to the clouds,
  Magnificence and wealth,
To reach a humbler, sweeter spot,
The village and the peaceful cot,
  The residence of health."   HOLLAND.

Let all who tread the green fields of Eyam remember, with feelings of awe and veneration, that beneath their feet repose the ashes of those moral heroes, who with a sublime, heroic, and an unparralelled resolution gave up their lives,—yea! doomed themselves to pestilential death, to save the surrounding country. The immortal victors of Thermopylæ and Marathon, who fought so bravely in liberty's holy cause, have no greater, no stronger, claim to the admiration of succeeding generations, than the humble villagers of Eyam in the year 1666. Their magnanimous self-sacrifice, in confining themselves within a proscribed boundary during the terrible pestilence, is unequalled in the annals of the world. The plague, which would undoubtedly have spread from place to place through the neighbouring counties, and which eventually carried off five-sixths of their number, was, in the following forcible language of a celebrated writer, " here hemmed in, and, in a dreadful and desolating struggle, destroyed and buried with its victims." How exalted, the sense of duty; how glorious the conduct of these children of nature, who, for the salvation of the country, heroically braved the horrors of certain, immediate, and pes-

tilential death. Tread softly, then, on the fields
where their ashes are laid; let the wild flowers
bloom on their wide-scattered graves. Let the
ground round the village be honoured and hallowed; for there,

"The dead are everywhere!
The mountain side; the plain; the woods profound;
All the lone dells—the fertile and the fair,
Is one vast burial ground." MARY HOWITT.

The desolation of Eyam by the plague, in the
years 1665 and 1666, (but more particularly in
1666,) has, from the time of its occurrence, always
been considered a most singular and remarkable
event: the more so as the ravages of the plague,
were far more dreadful and fatal at Eyam, according to its then population, than those of any other
pestilence hitherto recorded. From the latter end
of 1664 to December, 1665, about one-sixth of
the population of London fell victims to this appalling pestilence; but at Eyam, five-sixths were
carried off in a few months of the summer of 1666,
excepting a few who died at the close of 1665.
This dreadful scourge at Eyam has no parallel;
not even that of the "Black Death" of the fourteenth century.

Though the mortality of the Metropolis was
very great and horrible, yet there the populace
were not restrained as to flight; there they could
easily obtain medical aid; there neighbour knew
not neighbour; there thousands might die without
being intimately known to each other. But in
Eyam, a little sequestered village, containing about
three hundred and fifty stationary inhabitants, the
death of every one would be a neighbour, if not a
relative. In Eyam, then, the plague was, in the
language of Roberts, "the concentration of all
D 2

the more dreadful features of that visitation in London without its palliatives." Indeed, it seems exceeding strange, that Eyam, " a little mountain city, an insulated Zoar," secluded among the Peak mountains, distant from London 150 miles, should have been visited by a pestilential disease, which had scarcely ever occurred only in great and populous cities. It is, however, matter of fact, that this terrible plague was brought from London to Eyam in a box of old clothes and some tailors' patterns of cloth. Before I proceed to give the details of the commencement, progress, and horrible effects of this pestilence at Eyam, I shall take the liberty of noticing a few particulars respecting its cause, nature, symptoms, and whence it originated.

Pestilences in general are, as one writer remarks, a consequence of violent commotions in the earth, and are preceded by earthquakes, droughts, excessive rains, or pestiferous winds. Hecker observes, that at the time of the Black Death, in the fourteenth century, the foundations of the earth were shaken from China to the Atlantic ; and that through Europe and Asia the atmosphere, by its baneful influence, endangered both animal and vegetable life. The German Chroniclers inform us, that at this time a thick stinking mist advanced from the east, and spread itself over Italy ; and it is stated, that previously to an earthquake, at the same time, a pestiferous wind blew in Cyprus of such a deadly nature, that thousands fell down and expired in great agonies. Hecker further notices, that this is one of the rarest of phenomena, as Naturalists have never been able to discover foreign and pernicious ingredients in the air, almost desolating great portions of the earth, as in A.D. 1348. That the human body is a far more delicate test than philosophical instruments, the effects of the Egyptian Khamsin and the Italian Sirocco plainly and satisfactorily indicate. The Black Death of the fourteenth century, so called from the black spots or putrid decomposition of the skin, is stated to have carried off in the East 37,000,000 of human beings; and in Europe in proportion to its population. This destructive pestilence is beautifully described by Boccacio, in the introduction to his " Decameron."

But the most generally presumed efficient cause of contagious diseases, is a change in the proportions of the constituents of the atmosphere, affecting various artificial constituents. Infection and contagion have their origin in animalculæ; and, therefore, their infancy, maturity, and decline. The bubo of the plague is full of them. And Cooper says, " if this opinion be well founded it is no wonder that a chemical examination of the atmosphere cannot detect miasma, which does not depend on the state of the atmosphere." " Is not contagion," says Dr. Dwight, " such a fermentation of an animal body as generates animalculæ, and hence the danger of contact; and is not exemption after affection evidence that the germs in that subject have been exhausted. Sir Richard Phillips remarks, " that contagion is one of those words which, like attraction, suction, bewitching, and the like, mislead and obstruct inquiry." And he further observes, " that the differences concerning contagion among the faculty are intellectual phenomena."

The plague generally manifested itself by the febrile symptoms of shivering, nausea, headache, and delirium. In some these affections were so mild as to be taken for slight indisposition. The victim in this case generally attended his avocation until a sudden faintness came on, when the maculæ, or plague-spot, the fatal token, would soon appear on his breast, indicative of immediate death. But in most cases the pain and delirium left no room for doubt: on the second or third day buboes, or carbuncles, arose about the groin and elsewhere; and if they could be made to supporate, recovery was probable, but if they resisted the efforts of nature, and the skill of the physician, death was inevitable.

I may be pardoned for just observing, that even in the plague, the greatest enemy of the human race, there is a capriciousness, or rather something mysterious, which baffles even conjecture.

About the middle of the last century, Aleppo was visited by the plague, and one half of its inhabitants fell victims. The Rev. T. Dawes was then chaplain to the factory at Aleppo; and among many other particulars of the plague, he mentions the following very singular occurrences:—A woman was delivered of an affected child with the plague sores on its body, though the mother had been and was free from the distemper. Another woman that suckled her own child of five months old, was seized by the plague and died shortly after; but the child, though it suckled her, and lay in the same bed during her whole disorder, escaped the infection. And another woman, upwards of a hundred years old, was attacked with the plague, and recovered; but her two grandchildren of ten and sixteen years of age, received the infection from her, and both died.

Vinc. Fabricius relates, that when the plague raged in Holland, in 1636, a young girl was seized with it, had three buboes, and was removed to a garden, where her lover, who was betrothed to her,

attended her as a nurse, and slept with her as his
wife. He remained uninfected, and she (his beau-
teous Ægle) recovered, and was married to him—

———————————————" her plighted swain,
Soothes with soft kiss, with tender accents charms,
And clasps the bright infection in his arms."—DARWIN.

The following notices may be justly deemed cor-
roborative of the fact, that the plague was com-
municated from London to Eyam, in a box of
tailors' patterns of cloth. Mr. Williams, Chaplain
to Sir R. Suffon, formerly Ambassador at Con-
stantinople, relates that the jacket of a jannisary,
who had died of the plague, caused the death of
six more, who wore it in succession, before it was
ordered to be burned. Alexander Benedictus
mentions a feather bed, which proved mortal to
numbers on account of its being infected. Theo-
dore Mageire, in a paper laid before the King in
Council, at Paris, 1651, says, " that some ban-
dages of an infected person having been put between a wainscot and wall of a house in Paris,
gave the plague, a many years after, to a person
who took them out, and it spread immediately
through the city." Another writer observes, " that
contagious matter lodges most in goods of a loose
texture, which, being packed up and carried to
other countries, let out when opened the impri-
soned seeds of infection." At Florence, in 1348,
two hogs were seized with convulsions, and died
in less than an hour, through snuffling on some
rags which had been thrown into the street from a
poor man who had died of the plague. Forrester
states that seven children died by playing on
clothes brought from an infected house in Zealand
to Alkmull, North Holland. Thus, then, with
what wisdom and propriety, as we shall see subse-

quently, did Mompesson and the few survivors of
the plague at Eyam, burn almost every article of
clothing and furniture found in the village.

As to the sources of the plague there are different opinions. The general opinion is, that it is
propagated by contagion from the East. Pliny
insists that it is an African fever, bred in Ethiopia
or Egypt; and that it travels from South to North,
but more particularly West. Some maintain that
it is common to Europe, especially the South. It
is most probable, however, that there are different
kinds of epidemic diseases; or rather the plague
assumes different forms and aspects in different
countries and climates. The " Black Death" was
attended by expectoration of blood, the lungs being
attacked with carbuncular inflammation, which
must have added greatly to the fatality of the other
symptoms. After its first fury was spent, it assumed the usual form of the plague: hemorrhage
being no longer an attendant symptom. It was in
this form that it was brought by some ships from
Cyprus or Candia in the Levant, to Amsterdam
and Rotterdam, where it made horrible carnage in
the year 1663. Two Frenchmen are said to have
brought it in some woollen goods to London from
Holland, in December, 1664. These two Frenchmen, who resided in Longacre, London, on opening their goods, were seized with the plague and
died in a day or two in great agonies. Thus began, in London, this terrible scourge, which from
December, 1664, to the beginning of 1666, carried
off 100,000 souls.

During the dreadful ravages of the plague in
London, it is very probable that the then inhabitants of Eyam would hear but very little concerning that calamity. Confined to their secluded vil-

lage, which is surrounded by towering heath-clad hills, they were happily debarred from hearing at every turn that kind of intelligence which casts a gloom over the mind, or shocks the feelings. They were in a great measure unknown; health and plenty dwelt among them; and until the arrival of the fatal box, nothing had occurred to disturb "the even tenor of their way." Accompanied by simplicity and innocence, they sailed down the placid stream of rural life, unannoyed by the ever-fatal storms of avarice and ambition. Ah! up to this awful period they had lived in security and peace: attended by all the blessings of village life—

> " The life which those who fret in guilt,
> And guilty cities, never know; the life,
> Led by primeval ages, uncorrupt,
> When angels dwelt, and God himself, with Man !"
> THOMSON.

Before commencing the details of the arrival of the fatal box in Eyam, it may be interesting to know that the Eyam wakes of that year (1665) had only transpired a few days previously to that event: and it is said that this wakes was peculiarly marked by an unusual number of visitors, as if, as was imagined by the few survivors, these visitors, who were relatives to the villagers of Eyam, had been involuntarily moved to come and take a last farewell of those who were so very soon after destined to be swept away by the plague.* It is also said that the amusements on this occasion were more numerous and entertaining; but in what respect is not now known. Most probably, however,

---

* The wakes was held then when it ought to be—the first Sunday after the 18th of August, St. Helen's day. The time of holding the annual festival, or wakes, was changed to the last Sunday in August, about a century ago. The cause of this change was the harvest.

they would be of the usual and following character:—relations and friends would assemble at the
village alehouses, wishing each other as they raised
the sparkling glasses to their lips, many happy
returns of the festive time; the young men and
maidens would dance upon the spacious village
green; they would marry and be "given in marriage;" and numberless other innocent and social
amusements would close each gladsome, merry
day. Thus these fated beings would enjoy themselves on the brink of death: thus they would revel
in pleasure and mirth, unconscious of their speedy
doom! But, let me thus interrogate these children
of nature in their dust:—Were you not depressed
with sad and gloomy sensations? Were you not
moved by sudden and strange emotions? Did not
some oppressive and unaccountable weight rest on
your minds? Did not your lovely homes seem
conscious of some "mighty woe"? Did you not
behold over the village, DESOLATION written on the
sky? Did you not hear the awful footsteps of
approaching death? Did not the clouds weep
along the hills on that fatal day, when the pestilential box arrived, in which the invisible pest lay
concealed—in which that terrible minister of death
only slumbered awhile, to awake with greater
fury? Horrible was your doom! hapless children
of the hills! The struggle, however, is past, and
in the beautiful language of Ossian, shall not pos-
terity—

"Awake your memories in your tombs."

It is singular that all who have hitherto written
on this direful calamity, have invariably represented the plague as breaking out in Eyam, in the
spring of 1666. This, however, was not the case;

though by far the greater part of the number of victims died in July, August, and September, 1666. The box containing the tailor's patterns in cloth, and it is said some old clothes, was sent from London to a tailor who resided in a small house, at the west end of the church-yard, which has been rebuilded, and is now occupied by a Mr. S. Marsden. The kitchen of the old house is still as it was; it is only the house-place that has been renewed.* Whether the patterns and clothes were bought in London for the tailor at Eyam, or sent as a present, cannot now be ascertained. Some, however, say that it was a relative of the tailor at Eyam who sent them, he having procured them in London, where he resided, very cheaply in consequence of the plague, which was then raging there at its maximum. The box arrived at the tailor's house, Eyam, on the second or third of September, 1665. What the tailor's name was is not satisfactorily known: probably either Thrope or Cooper. The common belief is, that it was a man-servant, or journeyman tailor, who first opened the box, and not one of the family of the tailor, as is often stated. This is evident from the fact, that *Vicars,* the name of the first victim, does not occur again in the list of the names of the victims. And Dr. Mead, who lived a century nearer this occurrence than the present time, says the first victim was a servant. George Vicars, then, was the person who opened the terrible box. In removing the patterns and clothes, he observed in a sort of exclamation, how very damp they were; and he therefore hung them to the fire to dry. While

* In an old flue or chimney belonging to the kitchen of this house, a pair of old leather stays was found some years since. They were supposed to have been there ever since the plague; and were consequently buried with precipitation.

E

Vicars was superintending them he was suddenly
seized with violent sickness and other symptoms of
a disease, which greatly alarmed the family of the
house, and the neighbourhood. On the second
day he grew horribly worse: at intervals he was
delirious, and large swellings began to rise about
his neck and groin. What medical aid the village
afforded was procured, but to no avail. On the
third day of his illness the fatal token—the plague
spot—appeared on his breast, and he died in horrible agonies the following night, the sixth of September, 1665. The putrid state of his body rendered immediate interment necessary, and he was
interred in the church-yard the following day, September the seventh. Thus began, in Eyam, the
plague—the most awful of all diseases, which, after
being in some measure checked by the severity of
the following winter, began to spread amazingly,
and eventually left the village nearly desolate.

It is stated that the whole of the family of the
first victim, with the solitary exception of one, were
speedily carried off by the destructive pest. This,
however, is a mistake; for, according to the Register, the second victim, Edward, the son of Edward Cooper, was buried September twenty-second,
1666, after an interval of fourteen days. The remaining days of this month had almost each its victim; and the terrified villagers ascertained the fatal
disease to be the plague. Then!

> " Out it burst, a dreadful cry of death ;
> ' The Plague ! the Plague !' the withering language flew,
> And faintness followed on its rapid breath ;
> And all hearts sunk, as pierced with lightning through,
> ' The Plague ! the Plague ! no groundless panic grew ;
> But there, sublime in awful darkness, trod
> The pest ; and lamentation, as he slew,
> Proclaimed his ravage in each sad abode,
> Mid frenzied shrieks for aid—and vain appeals to God."
>   WILLIAM AND MARY HOWITT.

On the last day of September six persons had perished; and by the middle of October twelve more. Consternation and terror reigned throughout the village. The pestilence began to pass from house to house with increasing rapidity; the simple inhabitants looking forward with dreadful apprehension.

Some idea may be formed of the extreme virulence of the plague at Eyam, even at its commencement, by observing that even in large cities the plague has been known to cease in winter. In the first summer of the great plague, at Genoa, 10,000 died, in the winter scarcely any; but in the following summer, 60,000. The great plague in London first appeared in the latter end of 1664, but was checked by winter until the ensuing spring. While at Eyam, where the effects of winter would be considerably greater than in cities, the plague continued its ravages without ceasing. Still it did not attain the height of its destruction and malignancy until the summer of 1666.

Towards the latter end of October the pestilence increased; doleful lamentations issued from the cottages containing the infected persons; the distress of those families is unimaginable; few or none would visit them; they were avoided in the street; all dreaded coming in contact even with those belonging to the families where the infection reigned; they were glanced at with fearful apprehension, and their privations arising therefrom almost defy description. During this awful month twenty-two died. As winter approached the mortality became less, and hopes were entertained that the pestilence would cease. It continued, however, in spite of the weather, to pass from house to house, and in this month, November, seven died. In December, a great snow is said to have fallen, accompanied with a hard and severe frost. The distress of the inhabitants was very great; the pestilence rather increased, for nine died in December.

During the last four months of 1665, the sufferings of the villagers had been truly dreadful; and though they had become familiar with death, yet they were doomed, in the following summer, to behold the pest assume a far more deadly and fatal aspect. Though the then survivors had seen, in the above time, forty-four of their relatives and friends snatched from amongst them by the terrific hand of pestilential death, yet some few of them were destined to see double that number swept away in the short space of one month. Fated beings! shall not

" The bard preserve your names and send them down to future
    times?"—Ossian.

The weather at the commencement of 1666 was exceedingly cold and severe, which evidently diminished the baneful influence of the plague. Nothing could exceed the joy manifested by the villagers at there being, as they supposed, some prospect of being delivered from that scourge. The pestilence was now confined to two houses; and on the last day of January only four had died during that month. In February, however, eight died, and there were many affected.

I shall in this place, while the plague is the least furious, take the liberty of noticing some few particulars respecting the two unrivalled characters, who may be justly said to have been by their joint exertions, the principal instruments by whom Derbyshire and the neighbouring counties were delivered from the desolating plague,—the Rev. Thomas Stanley and the Rev. William Mompesson.

We shall see when we come to the time of the greatest fury of the plague, that the salvation of the surrounding country, originated in the wisdom of these two worthy divines. Their magnanimous conduct on this awful occasion can only be exceeded by the obedience of the sufferers over whom they exercised such heavenly influence. "One can scarcely decide," says Mr. Samuel Roberts, " in this case, which most to admire, the wisdom of the pastor, or the obedience of his flock. It was a sacrifice in either case, which we are utterly unable duly to appreciate. I can form no conception of any instance, in mere human beings, more strongly proving the blessed effects of true Christianity than this, of faith no stronger, no obedience more perfect." The same writer thus very justly observes :—" Ought not a monument to have been erected, by the nation, to the memory of all those who fell victims, and a liberal national annuity to have been granted to each of the heroic survivors. They have, however, monuments to their memories, in the hearts of all truly good and sympathizing men."

The Rev. Thomas Stanley was born at Duckmanton, near Chesterfield. His public ministry was exercised at Handsworth, Dore, and eight years at Ashford, whence, by those in power, he was translated, in 1644, to the rectory of Eyam, where he continued to reside, respected, esteemed, and loved until Bartholomew-day, 1662. He continued to preach, however, in private houses at Eyam, Hazleford, and other places, until his death, in 1670. This very worthy man was succeeded by his predecessor, the Rev. Sherland Adams, who died in 1664. The successor of this litigious divine, was the Rev. William Mompesson,

chaplain to Sir George Saville. Before his coming
to Eyam, in April, 1664, he had married a beautiful young lady, Catherine, the daughter of Ralph
Carr, Esq., of Cocken, in the county of Durham.
She was young and possessed good parts, with ex-
quisitely tender feelings. These two illustrious
characters (Stanley and Mompesson) throughout
the fury of the pestilence, as we shall see hereafter,
forsook not their flock, but visited, councilled, and
exhorted them in their sufferings; alleviated their
miseries, and held fast to their duties on the very
threshold of death.

On the first of March, 1666, the plague had
carried off fifty-six souls; and during this month
but little abatement was perceived in the number
infected. Six died in this month. In the succeeding month April, nine; and in May, three.
This seeming relaxation of fury in the latter month,
inspired the trembling villagers with a ray of de-
lusive hope: they began to ascribe the past malignancy of the pest to the severity of the winter,
and the fearful dismay which had oppressed their
drooping spirits, began to subside. But, alas!
while these innocent and simple beings were indulging in this vain dream, the plague, that subtle
and mysterious minister of death, was only resting
and gathering strength to make more horrible
slaughter. At the commencement of June this
deadly monster awoke from his short slumber; and
with desolating steps stalked forth from house to
house, breathing on the terror-struck inhabitants,
the vapour of death. The irresistible rage of the
pest filled the hearts of the trembling villagers with
dreadful forebodings: despair seized every soul.
Loud and bitter lamentations burst forth from
every infected house! Fear and apprehension

prevented ingress to these abodes of distress.
Horror and dismay enveloped the village! The
extreme dread even of the uninfected, led them to
the practice of a thousand weak and absurd expe-
dients, to prevent them from taking the distemper.
Numberless omens and presages of their dreadful
calamities, the terrified inhabitants could now call
to mind. Some said that the desolation of the
village had been at various times prognosticated.
Many could recollect having seen the white cricket,
and heard it sound the death-knell on their hearths.
Others remembered having heard for three successive nights the invisible "death-watch" in the
dead of night. And some called to mind how
often during a few preceding winters they had
listened to the doleful howlings of the Gabriel-
hounds.

These, with numerous other fanciful tokens of
death, these simple and horrified villagers imagined
at this awful time they had seen and heard. Nor
would it have been marvellous, had they imagined
they beheld with Ossian's Melilcoma, "the awful
faces of other times looking from the clouds."

As June advanced, the pestilence spread from
house to house with dreadful rapidity; sparing
neither sex nor age.

"Health, strength, and infancy, and age
In vain the ruthless foe engage."—HOLLAND.

The unexampled mortality of the plague during
the summer of 1666, is, as I have before stated,
unequalled in history. Some have supposed that
this destructive scourge was aggravated to its un-
paralleled fury at Eyam by the ignorance and des-
titution of the inhabitants; and their consequent
maltreatment of the distemper. Others have conjectured that it was aided in its dreadful career by

the hotness of the summer; this season being in
those times, in the Peak, more sultry, but much
shorter. This change is said to have arisen from
the extensive inclosures, and the spirited cultiva-
tion of the surrounding moors. But the proximate
cause of this unheard of mortality was undoubtedly
the courageous determination of the villagers to
confine themselves within a certain boundary; for
if those who fell a sacrifice in July, August, September, and October, had fled in the spring, they
would most probably have escaped; but then there
was this danger, had they not taken that magnanimous step :—the infected would have fled with the
non-infected, and thereby have carried desolation
wherever they went. Hence, I imagine, we may
trace the principal and efficient cause of that horrible carnage among the meritorious villagers of
Eyam.

Up to the beginning of June seventy-four had
perished from the commencement of the pest;
this number of deaths, from a population of 350,
was very great in so short a time; but, how incomparable to the dreadful havoc of the ensuing
months of June, July, August, September, and
October.

It was about the middle of June, that the plague
began to assume so terrible an aspect. Terror
overwhelmed the hearts of the villagers. Mrs.
Mompesson threw herself and two children, George
and Elizabeth, of three and four years old, at the
feet of her husband, imploring their immediate
departure from the devoted place! Her entreaties
and tears sensibly moved the feelings of her husband. But Mompesson, whose love for his wife
and children was never exceeded, whose eyes were
suffused with tears by this energetic and truly

pathetic appeal, raised her from his feet, and in
the most affectionate manner, told her, that his
duty to his suffering and diminishing flock—that
the indelible stain that would rest on his memory
by deserting them in the hour of danger—and that
the awful responsibility to his Maker, for the charge
he had undertaken, were considerations with him
of more weight and importance than life itself!
He then again, in the most enthusiastic manner,
endeavoured to prevail on his weeping partner to
take their two lovely babes and fly to some place
of refuge until the plague was stayed! She, however, steadfastly resisted his persuasions, and emphatically declared her determination that nothing
should induce her to leave him amidst that destructive and terrible whirlpool of death! This affecting
contest ended in their mutual consent to send the
children away to a relative in Yorkshire, (supposed to be J. Beilby, Esq.,) until the pestilence
ceased. There is a tradition of the mournful
parting of the children and parents on this occasion. Mompesson called them aside, and, sup-
pressing the bitterness of his feelings, gave each a
parting kiss, and fervently admonished them to be
obedient and good! Their tender and loving
mother grasped each in her arms, and in the
intervals of heart-bursting sighs kissed them
again and again! When they departed, she ran
to the highest window of their dwelling and watched
them leave the village. As she caught the last
glance of them, a sudden and startling thought
crossed her mind that she should behold them no
more! She uttered a shrill and piercing scream!
Mompesson hastened to her side and endeavoured
to console her in the most soothing language
imaginable! In the first paroxysm of her grief

she intently gazed towards the spot where they
last met her view; nor would she be removed from
the place, until the streaming tears

"Rushed from her clouded brain,
Like mountain mists, at length dissolved to rain."

BYRON.

Alas! alas! her forebodings were realised: in
this world she beheld her children no more: she
took the infection, and died, as we shall hereafter
see, blessing her children with her last parting
breath!

It was at this period of the calamity (about the
middle of June) that the inhabitants began to
think of escaping from death by flight. Indeed,
the most wealthy of them, who were but few in
number, fled early in the spring with the greatest
precipitation. Some few others, having means,
fled to the neighbouring hills and dells, and there
erected huts; and dwelled therein, until the ap-
proach of winter. But it was the visible manifes-
tation of a determination in the whole mass to flee,
that aroused Mompesson; he energetically remonstrated with them on the danger of flight; he told
them of the fearful consequences that would ensue;
that the safety of the surrounding country was in
their hands; that it was impossible for them to
escape death by flight; that a many of them were
infected; that the invisible seeds of the disease
lay concealed in their clothing and other articles
they had prepared to take with them; and that if
they would relinquish their fatal and terrible purpose, he would write to all the influential persons
in the vicinity for aid; he would by every possible
means in his power endeavour to alleviate their
sufferings; and he would remain with them, and
sacrifice his life rather than be instrumental in

desolating the surrounding country! Thus spoke
this wonderful man! Let us, however, hear his
entreaties on this awful occasion in the words of
the poet :—

" Alas! beloved friends! Alas! where strays
Your wonted mind? What means these signs of flight?
Is God unpitying, though He wrath displays?
Is the sun quenched when clouds obscure his light?
Oh! calm your trembling souls, be strong in Christian might.
Here we may strive and conquer, and may save
Our country from this desolating curse;
Some few, perchance, may fill an earlier grave;
But, if ye fly. it follows, and ye nurse
Death in your flight; wide, wider ye disperse
Destruction through the land. Oh, then! bow down
And vow to Him to virtue ne'er averse,
To stand unshrinking 'neath death's fiercest frown.
Then Heaven shall give us rest, and earth a fair renown."

WILLIAM AND MARY HOWITT.

The inhabitants, with a superhuman courage,
gave up all thoughts of flight. Mompesson, immediately wrote to the Earl of Devonshire, then
at Chatsworth, a few miles from Eyam, stating
the particulars of the calamity, and adding that he
was certain, that he could prevail on his suffering
and hourly diminishing flock, to confine themselves
within the precincts of the village if they could be
supplied with victuals and other necessary articles,
and thereby prevent the pestilence from spreading.
The Noble Earl expressed in his answer, deep
commiseration for the sufferers; and he further
assured Mompesson, that nothing should be spared
on his part, to mitigate the calamitous sufferings
of the inhabitants—provided they kept themselves
within a specified bound. This worthy Nobleman,
who remained at Chatsworth during the whole
time of the plague, generously ordered the sufferers to be supplied with all kinds of necessaries,
agreeably to the following plan.

A kind of circle was drawn round the village, marked by particular and well known stones and hills; beyond which it was solemnly agreed that no one of the villagers should proceed, whether infected or not. This circle extended about half a mile around the village; and at two or three places or points of this boundary, provisions were brought. The places on the circle were appointed in different directions, in order that the pestilential effluvia might not be directed all in one way, by those set apart to fetch the articles left, and who might be infected. A well, or rivulet, northward of Eyam, called to this day, "Mompesson's Well," or "Mompesson's Brook," was one of the places where articles were deposited. These articles were brought very early in the morning, by persons from the adjoining villages, who, when they had delivered them beside the well, fled with the precipitation of panic. Persons set apart by Mompesson and Stanley fetched the articles left; and when they took money, it was deposited in the Well and certain distant troughs, to be purified, and to prevent contagion by passing from hand to hand. The persons who brought the articles were careful to wash the money well before they took it away. An account was left at this and other places of the progress of the disease, the number of deaths, and other particulars. When money was sent, it was only for some extra or particular articles: the provisions and many other necessaries were supplied, it is generally asserted, by the Earl of Devonshire.—The Cliffe, between Stoney Middleton and Eyam, was another place on the circle appointed for this purpose. A large vessel of water stood there, in which money and other things were deposited for purifi-

cation. There are other places of this sort pointed
out, but these were the most particular.

It is said that no one ever crossed this *cordon
sanitaire* from within or without, during the awful
calamity: this, however, is not precisely correct.
One person, as we shall see hereafter, crossed it
from without at the sacrifice of life; and in a subsequent part I shall give some interesting particulars of some who crossed it from within. It
must be granted, however, that it was to the pre-
scribing of this boundary and other precautions
attendant thereon, that the country around was
saved from this most horrible pestilence. The
wisdom of Mompesson, who is said to have originated this plan, can only be surpassed in degree
by the courage of the inhabitants in not trespass-
ing beyond the bounds prescribed, whom, as Miss
Seward justly observes, "a cordon of soldiers
could not have prevented against their will, much
less could any watch which might have been set
by the neighbourhood, have effected that important purpose." The annals of mankind afford no
instance of such magnanimous conduct in a joint
number of persons." And ages pass away without being honoured by such an immortal character
as Mompesson, who, while the black sword of pestilence was dealing death around him, voluntarily
"put his life in his hand," from an exalted sense
of duty,—for the salvation of the country. Towards the latter end of June, the plague began to
rage more fearfully. Nothing but lamentations
were heard in the village. The passing bell ceased,
the church yard was no longer resorted to for interment, and the church door closed.

> " Contagion closed the portal of the fane
> In which he wont the bread of life to deal;
> He then a temple sought, not made with hands,
> But reared by Him, amidst whose works it stood
> Rudely magnificent."　　　　　　Rogers.

F

Mompesson, at this juncture, deeming it dangerous to assemble in the Church during the hot weather, proposed to meet his daily diminishing flock
in the Delf, a secluded dingle a little south of
Eyam, and there read prayers twice a week, and
deliver his customary sermons on the Sabbath,
from a perforated arch in an ivy-mantled rock.
The ghastly hearers seated themselves at some
distance from each other on the grassy slope, opposite the rocky pulpit. Thither they assembled
one by one for many a Sabbath morn, leaving at
their mournful homes, some a father, some a mother, some a brother, and some a child struggling
with death. They glanced at each other with
looks of unutterable woe, asking in silence, " whom
Fate would next demand." Mompesson, from the
massive cut, lifted up his voice to heaven and
called aloud on the God of mercy to stay
the deadly pest, while the fervent responses
of the shuddering hearers dolefully echoed from
the caverns around. Thus they assembled in the
sacred dell, while each succeeding Sabbath told
the horrid work of death. " Do you not see,"
says Miss Seward, " this dauntless minister of
God stretching forth his hand from the rock, in-
structing and consoling his distressed flock in that
little wilderness? How solemn, how affecting,
must have been the pious exhortations of these
terrible hours." Rhodes observes, " that Paul
preaching at Athens, or John the Baptist in the
wilderness, scarcely excites a more powerful and
solemn interest than this minister of God, this
' legate of the skies,' when contemplated on this
trying occasion, ' when he stood between the dead
and living, and the plague was stayed.' " Numbers, chap. 16, verse 48. This romantic arch has,
from that terrible time, always been designated
" Cucklett Church." How insensible to the

awfulness of that horrible season must be that
being who can tread this hallowed dell and not hear

" Amidst the rocks an awful sound
  In deep reverberation sigh,
And all the echoing caverns round
  With mournful voices far reply,
As if, in those sepulchral caves,
  The dead were speaking from their graves."
                                        BRETTELL.

Few or no instances are on record, of the extinction of life in a joint number of mortals, attended with such trying and appalling circumstances as the plague at Eyam, in July, August,
and September, 1666. During these dreadful
months, the terrific sufferings of the inhabitants
almost defy description. Parents beheld their
children fall in direful succession by the hand of
the insatiable and purple-visaged pest. Children
turned aside with fearful dread at the distorted
features of their parents in death. Every family
while they were any left, buried their own dead;
and one hapless woman, in the space of a few days,
as we shall hereafter see, dug the graves for, and
buried with her own hands, her husband and six
children. Appalling as such a circumstance must
be, it is, however, only one of a very many of that
dreadful time.

We are now arriving at the period when the
fury of the pestilence attained its maximum: when
it threatened the terrified villagers with utter ex-
termination. Fear and dismay overshadowed their
souls; they shrunk back with terror at the increasing ravages of this most capricious, indescribable,
and horrid disease; which, in the beautiful language of the poet,—

" Darts in the whirlwind—floats upon the breeze—
Creeps down the vales, and hangs upon the trees—

Strikes in a sunbeam—in the evening cool—
Flags on the fog, and stagnates on the pool—
In films ætherial, taints the vital air—
Steals through a pore, and creeps along a hair—
Invades the eye in light—the ear in sounds—
Kills with a touch, and at a distance wounds."—FURNESS.

A few of the last days of June were exceedingly hot, and the infection spread with horrible rapidity. The Church-yard closed its gates against the dead. Funeral rites were no longer read; coffins and shrouds were no longer thought off; an old door or chair was at first the bier on which the dead were borne; and a half-made grave or hole hastily dug in the fields and gardens round the cottages, received each putrid corpse ere life was quite extinct. With the commencement of July, the weather became extremely warm and sultry; and the rage of the pest really terrific. Dreadful wailings burst forth from every side; and the countenances of the few who ventured abroad were deeply impressed with the visible signs of inward horror. The village was unfrequented; it stood, as it were out of the world; none came to sympathise with its suffering inhabitants: no traveller passed through the lonely street during that awful time: it was regarded and avoided, as the valley of death! Horror and Destruction rode, and marked the boundary of the dreadful place. On the clouds that hung gloomily over the village were written "Pestilence and Death:" at which terrific inscription, the approaching stranger turned aside and precipitately fled; haunted and chased by horrid and terrible fears. Thus, helpless and alone, perished the villagers of Eyam, for the salvation of the country :—

"Struck by turns, in solitary pangs
They fell, unblest, untended, and unmourn'd."— THOMSON.

It is impossible for pen to describe, or imagination to conceive, the unspeakable distress of those who resided in that part of the village, and in those houses, where the plague raged from first to last, with the greatest violence. Some dwellings in July, and especially in August, contained at one moment both the dying and the dead. In one individual house, a victim was struggling with death, while they were hurrying another therefrom to a grave in the fields. In another, a few were anxiously watching and wishing for the last convulsive gasp, that the victim might be instantly interred, and that "so much of the disease might be buried, and its influence destroyed." The open day witnessed the putrid bodies of the victims pass along the street; and sable night was startled at the frequent footsteps of the buriers of the dead. The horrid symptom of the last stage of the disease in almost every victim, was the signal for the digging of a grave, or rather hole, to which the deceased, placed on the first thing at hand, or more often dragged on the ground, was speedily hurried and buried with inconceivable precipitation; "even whilst the limbs were yet warm, and almost palpitating with life." So anxious were they for immediate interment, that some were buried close by their cottage doors, and it is said, some in the back parts of the very houses in which they died. In this state of things passed day after day, and week after week. The terrified villagers had for some time forsaken their wonted occupations; the untended cattle lowed mournfully on the neighbouring hills; the fields and gardens became a wilderness; and family feuds and personal animosities sank in oblivion! Nothing was now scarcely seen, save—

" The deep-racking pang, the ghastly form,

The lip pale-quivering, and the beamless eye
No more with ardour bright."   THOMSON.

Every family up to July had been from dire
necessity compelled to bury their own dead; for
no one would touch, nor even glance at a corpse
that did not belong to his own house or family.
But when, as was now frequently the case, the last
of a family died, or when one died in a house and
the others were dying, some person was neces-
sitated, however dangerous the task, to undertake
the charge of removing the unsightly corpse, and
instantly burying it. For this hazardous but
necessary purpose, the All-wise Providence had
endowed with sufficient nerve, hardihood, and in-
difference the person of Marshall Howe, a man of
gigantic stature, a native of the village, and of a
most courageous calibre. The daring conduct of
this individual in that terrible time, has rendered
his name familiar with the villagers of Eyam to the
present day. During the greatest fury of the
plague, he filled the fearful office of burier of the
dead. It appears, however, that he took the distemper nearly at the time of its first appearance,
but recovered; and from a belief that a person
was never attacked twice, much of his intrepidity
may be ascribed. Covetousness, or avarice, seems
to have instigated him in part, to undertake his
perilous vocation. When he learned that some
one was dying, without relatives to take charge
of interment, he immediately proceeded to a garden or adjoining field, and opened a grave; then
he hastened to the house where the victim lay still
warm with life, and tying one end of a cord round
the neck of the corpse, he threw the other over his
shoulder and dragged it forth through the street to
the grave, and with an "unhallowed haste" lightly

covered it with earth. The money, furniture, clothes, and other effects of the deceased were his unenviable remuneration. For near three months he was thus employed. By some, however, he was paid a stipulated sum for interring their deceased relatives; acquiring in this manner both money and valuables. Through burying the last victims of the pest houses, he took and claimed whatever he found therein; and in alluding to the quantity of clothing he had thus obtained, he jocularly observed, that "he had pinners and napkins sufficient to kindle his pipe with while he lived." Such was the awful occupation of Marshall Howe during the most horrible ravages of the plague; he, however, tasted the bitter draught, by burying with his own hands, his wife on the twenty-seventh, and his son on the thirtieth of August of the fatal 1666. For a generation or two after the plague, parents in Eyam endeavoured to bring their children to rule and obedience by telling them that they would send for Marshall Howe.

A few of the last days of July were really dreadful; sometimes five, sometimes six died in one day; and in the whole month fifty-seven. But it was in August that the pest bared his arm for the most deadly slaughter. The weather became in this month remarkably hot, and the pestilence spread throughout the village. Distraction overwhelmed the hourly diminishing villagers; some lay in a death-like stupor, anticipating their doom; others ran about the street in a state of madness, until they suddenly dropped down dead. From every house that was not empty, loud and dismal cries issued forth, mixed with violent exclamations of pain; and as Ossian sings, "the groan of the people spread over the hills." The swellings in the neck and groin of the patient became insufferable when they would not burst, and the torment was unspeakably excruciating. All now expected death; no one cherished a hope of escaping; and a mournful gloom settled on the features of the few who ventured to pace the lonely street. Those who fetched from the stated places the victuals and other articles were marked on the brow by sullen despair; and even

> " The very children had imbibed a look
> Of such unutterable woe, as told
> A tale of sorrows indescribable."   Roberts.

As August advanced, the mortality increased with inconceivable rapidity. The wakes came on again, but alas! alas! how awful the change. The remaining few thought not of their wonted joy; they breathed not its name, for all their thoughts were full of death! The festive Sunday passed away, with all the stillness of the grave; none watched for the arrival of relations and friends; no village choristers assembled at the church; nor did the cheerful bells call aloud to the hills to be merry and glad. Nearly all who had tripped upon the village-green, at the last anniversary of this till then happy time, were now, uncoffined, laid in their graves.

Towards the latter end of the fatal month, near four-fifths of the inhabitants were swept away. Mompesson, during the whole time, unremittingly went from house to house comforting, as much as possible, his dying flock. He, however, was an ailing man, and had an issue in his leg. One day his beloved wife observed a green ichor issuing from the wound, which she conceived to be the result of his having taken the distemper, and its having found a vent that way. Great was her joy

on this occasion; and though Mompesson thought
she was mistaken, yet he, as we shall see in his
letter to his children, fully and duly appreciated
her extreme anxiousness for his welfare. This admirable and worthy man was now destined to drink
of the sickening cup which had been passing round
the village. Catherine, his beloved partner, had,
during the spring, shown symptoms of a pulmonary
consumption. She is represented to have been
exceedingly beautiful though very delicate. There
is a very current tradition in the village, that on
the morning of the twenty-second of August, 1666,
Mompesson and his wife walked out arm in arm in
the fields adjoining the Rectory, as had been their
custom for some months in the spring, hoping that
the morning air would restore her convalescency.
During this walk she had been dwelling on her
usual theme—her two absent children, when, just
as they were leaving the last field for their habitation, she suddenly exclaimed: " Oh ! Mompesson ! the air ! how sweet it smells !" These words
went through the very soul of Mompesson, and his
heart sunk within him ! He made some evasive
reply, and they entered their dwelling. The lapse
of a few hours confirmed his fearful anticipation
from her remark in the fields : she had taken the
distemper, the horrid symptoms appeared, she became at intervals delirious, and before night no
hope was entertained of her recovery. Mompesson seemed for awhile unable to stand the terrible
shock; distraction overwhelmed him, and he stood
at her bedside a statue of despair. He, however,
after the first paroxysm of grief was past, began,
with a fortitude unexampled, to use every means
imaginable to arrest the progress of the disease.
Cordials and chemical antidotes were administered

by his own hand; but, alas! in vain. She struggled with the invincible pest until the morning of the twenty-fourth, when her spirit took its flight to the regions of bliss. Mompesson cast himself beside her putrid corpse; and in the agony of despair bathed her cold and pallid face with burning tears. The domestics came and led him faltering away; yet ere he left the room he turned, and, sobbing, cried "farewell! farewell! all happy days!" He repaired to his closet, and on his bended knees lifted up his voice to heaven; while,

> " One lightning-winged cry
> Shot through the hamlet; and a wailing grew,
> Wilder than when the plague-fiend first drew nigh,
> One troublous hour,—and from all quarters fly
> The wretched remnant, who had ceased to weep;
> But sorrow, which had drained their bosoms dry,
> Found yet fresh fountains in the spirit deep,
> Wringing out burning tears that loved one's couch to steep."
> WILLIAM AND MARY HOWITT.

She who had been a few days past so lovely and beautiful, was now a livid corpse; she who had been the object of every attention, now lay lone and still, guarded from every eye by dreadful apprehension.

> " Ah! then Mompesson felt
> What human tongue nor poet's pen must feign—
> Quick to the grave the kindred earth was given
> With e'en affection's last sad pledge forgone,
> The mortal kiss—for round those blighted lips,
> Exaled the ling'ring spirit of the pest,
> As if in triumph o'er all that was once
> So lovely and beloved."
> HOLLAND.

Thus, this lovely and amiable woman fell a victim to the plague in the twenty-seventh year of her age. Her resolution to abide with her husband in defiance of death, is a striking instance of the strength and purity of female affection. She was interred the day after her death, August, the twenty-fifth, 1666, in the church-yard at Eyam. Over her ashes her loving and truly affectionate husband erected a splendid tomb, which, with its inscription and devices, will be described hereafter.

Great as was the calamity that had visited and was still visiting almost every family in the fated village : terrible as was the devastation of the pestilence in August, yet the very few inhabitants that were left nearly forgot their own sufferings and distress in the death of Mrs. Mompesson. They had witnessed in her worthy husband, so much sympathy and benevolence, so much attention and human feeling, that they regarded him as their counsellor, physician, and friend, and hence their participation in his sorrow for the loss of his lovely and amiable wife. The trying situation, the lacerated sensations of this incomparable man will be best shown by the two following letters, written with his own hand a few days after the interment of his affectionate spouse.

To his dear children he thus announces the death of their mother :—

" To my dear children, George and Elizabeth Mompesson, these present with my blessing.
" Eyam, August 31, 1666.

" DEAR HEARTS,—This brings you the doleful news of your dear mother's death—the greatest loss which ever befel you ! I am not only deprived of a kind and loving consort, but you also are bereaved of the most indulgent mother that ever dear children had. We must comfort ourselves in God with this consideration, that the loss is only ours, and that what is our sorrow is her gain. The consideration of her joys, which I do assure myself are unutterable, should refresh our drooping spirits.

" My children, I think it may be useful to you to have a narrative of your dear mother's virtues, that the knowledge thereof may teach you to imitate her excellent qualities. In the first place, let me recommend to you her piety and devotion, which were according to the exact principles of the Church of England. In the next place, I can assure you, she was composed of modesty and humility, which virtues did possess her dear soul in a most exemplary manner. Her discourse was ever grave and meek, yet pleasant also; an immodest word was never heard to come from her mouth. She had two other virtues, modesty and frugality. She never valued any thing she had, when the necessities of a poor neighbour required it; but had a bountiful spirit towards the distressed and indigent; yet she was never lavish, but commendably frugal. She never liked tattling women, and abhorred the custom of going from house to house, thus wastefully spending precious time. She was ever busied in useful work, yet, though prudent, she was affable and kind. She avoided those whose company could not benefit her, and would not unbosom herself to such, still she dismissed them with civility. I could tell you of her many other excellent virtues. I do believe, my dear hearts, that she was the kindest wife in the world, and think from my soul, that she loved me ten times better than herself; for she not only resisted my entreaties, that she should fly with you, dear children, from this place of death, but, some few days before it pleased God to visit my house, she perceived a green matter to come from the issue in my leg, when she fancied a symptom that the distemper, raging amongst us, had found a vent that way, whence she assured herself that I was passed the malignity of the disorder, whereat she rejoiced exceedingly, not considering her own danger thereby. I think, however, that she was mistaken in the nature of the discharge she saw: certainly it was the salve that made it look so green; yet her rejoicing was a strong testimony that she cared not for her own peril so I were safe.

" Further, I can assure you, that her love to you was little inferior than to me; since why should she thus ardently desire my long continuance in this world of sorrows, but that you might have the protection and comfort of my life. You little imagine with what delight she talked of you both, and the pains she took when you suckled your milk from her breasts. She gave strong testimony of her love for you when she lay on her death-bed. A few hours before she expired I wished her to take some cordials, which she told me plainly she could not take. I entreated she would attempt for your dear sakes. At the mention of your names, she with difficulty lifted up her head and took them: this was to testify to me her affection for you.

" Now I will give you an exact account of the manner of her death. For some time she had shown symptoms of a consumption, and was wasted thereby. Being surrounded by infected families, she doubtless got the distemper from them; and her natural strength being impaired, she could not struggle with the disease, which made her illness so very short. She showed much contrition for the errors of her past life, and often cried out,—' One drop of my Saviour's blood, to save my soul.' She earnestly desired me not to come near her, lest I should receive harm thereby; but, thank God, I did not desert her, but stood to my resolution not to leave her in her sickness, who had been so tender a nurse to me in her health. Blessed be God, that He enabled me to be so helpful and consoling to her, for which she was not a little thankful. During her illness she was not disturbed by worldly business—she only minded making her call and election sure; and she asked pardon of her maid, for having sometimes given her an angry word. I gave her some sweating antidotes, which rather inflamed her more, whereupon her dear head was distempered, which put her upon many incoherencies. I was troubled thereat, and propounded to her questions in divinity. Though in all other things she talked at random, yet to these religious questions, she gave me as rational answers as could be desired. I bade her repeat after me certain prayers, which she did with great devotion,—it gave me comfort that God was so gracious to her.

" A little before she died, she asked me to pray with her again. I asked her how she did? The answer was, that she was looking when the good hour should come. Thereupon I prayed, and she made her responses from the Common Prayer Book, as perfectly as in her health, and an ' Amen' to every pathetic expression. When we had ended the prayers for the sick, we used those from the Whole Duty of Man! and when I heard her say nothing, I said, ' My dear, dost thou mind ?' She answered, ' Yes,' and it was the last word she spoke.

" My dear babes, the reading of this account will cause many a salt tear to spring from your eyes; yet let this comfort you—your mother is a saint in heaven.

" Now, to that blessed God, who bestowed upon her all ' those graces,' be ascribed all honour, glory, and dominion, the just tribute of all created beings, for evermore.—Amen !

" WILLIAM MOMPESSON."

Is there not in this truly pathetic letter, the visible effusion of a purely Christian spirit,—the bright effulgence of a heavenly mind, which shall command the admiration of succeeding generations, to the end of time? On the same melancholy event, the following letter was written by Momesson, to his friend and patron, Sir George Saville :—

" Eyam, September 1, 1666.

" HONOURED AND DEAR SIR,—This is the saddest news that ever my pen could write! The destroying Angel having taken up his quarters within my habitation, my dearest wife is gone to her eternal rest, and is invested with a crown of righteousness, having made a happy end. Indeed, had she loved herself as well as me, she had fled from the pit of destruction with the sweet babes, and might have prolonged her days; but she was resolved to die a martyr to my interests. My drooping spirits are much refreshed with her joys, which I think are unutterable.

" Sir, this paper is to bid you a hearty farewell for ever, and to bring you my humble thanks for all your noble favours; and I hope you will believe a dying man, I have as much love as honour for you, and I will bend my feeble knees to the God of Heaven, that you, my dear lady, and your children and their children, may be blessed with external and eternal happiness, and that the same blessing may fall upon Lady Sunderland and her relations.

" Dear Sir, let your dying Chaplain recommend this truth to you and your family, that no happiness or solid comfort can be found in this vale of tears, like living a pious life; and pray ever remember this rule, *never do anything upon which you dare not first ask the blessing of God.*

" Sir, I have made bold in my will with your name for executor, and I hope you will not take it ill. I have joined two others with you, who will take from you the trouble. Your favourable aspect will, I know, be a great comfort to my distressed orphans. I am not desirous that they should be great, but good; and my next request is, that they be brought up in the fear and admonition of the Lord.

" Sir, I thank God I am contented to shake hands with all the world; and have many comfortable assurances that God will accept me through his Son. I find the goodness of God greater than I ever thought or imagined; and I wish from my soul that it were not so much abused and continued. I desire, Sir, that you will be pleased to make choice of a humble, pious man, to succeed me in my parsonage; and could I see your face before my departure hence, I would inform you in what manner I think he may live comfortable amongst his people, which would be some satisfaction to me before I die.

" Dear Sir, I beg the prayers of all about you that I may not be daunted by the powers of hell; and that I may have dying graces: with tears I beg, that when you are praying for fatherless orphans, you would remember my two pretty babes.

" Pardon the rude style of this paper, and be pleased to believe that I am, dear Sir, &c.

" WILLIAM MOMPESSON."

" In the whole range of literature," says William and Mary Howitt, " we know of nothing more pathetic than these letters ;" alluding, besides these two, to another, dated Eyam, Nov. 20, 1666, which will be found hereafter.

It is singular, indeed, that Mompesson enjoyed such remarkable good health during the whole time of the calamitous visitation : he, in the language of the poet,

" Drew, like Marseilles' good bishop, purer breath,
When nature sickened, and each gale was death."

From house to house he went, and prayed with the dying victims :—

" Beside the bed where parting life was laid,
And sorrow, guilt, and pain, by turns dismayed,
The reverend champion stood." GOLDSMITH.

From the interment of Mrs. Mompesson (August the twenty-fifth) to the end of the month, the pestilence raged with unabated fury: although four-fifths of the population were swept away. On the twenty-sixth of this terrible month, Marshall Howe, who had been daily employed in hurrying the dead to their unhallowed graves, was doomed to experience a loss, equal in his own estimation to that of his pastor. Joan his wife, who had often remonstrated with him to desist from his perilous avocation, was seized with the distemper : and the virulence of the attack threatened almost immediate dissolution. Though he had been, for full two months, moving in the whirlwind of death, yet up to this time, he had doomed himself invulnerable to the pest; but the infection of his wife brought conviction to his mind, that he had been the means of bringing the disease across his own threshold ; and he wept bitterly. The direful symptom appeared on the snow-white bosom of his beloved Joan : and early on the morning of the twenty-seventh she breathed her last. Marshall wept aloud over her stiffening limbs; but ere the sun had tipped with gold the orient hills of Eyam, he wound her up and carried her in his brawny arms to a neighbouring field, where he dug a grave and placed her silently therein. A sullen sadness overspread his mien, while over her remains he patted the earth with an unusual and unconscious circumspection. Filled with gloomy sensations he returned to his home, but, alas ! there he found his only, his dearest son William, struggling with the pest. Despair " whirled his brain to madness :" he cast himself on a couch and uttered doleful lamentations. William, his beloved son, who had inherited something of his father's iron constitution, wrestled with the horrid and deadly monster until the morning of the third day of his sickness, when he yielded to his direful and mortal antagonist. His disconsolate father bore his warm but lifeless corpse to the grave of his wife, beside which he buried it, while floods of tears bespoke his inconceivable agony. The necessity, however, of Marshall Howe, compelled him to continue in the office of burier of the dead. But the recklessness and levity which he had exhibited were no longer observable after the bereavement of his wife and son. The terrified and fast dwindling villagers were no longer startled, when he returned from the interment of a victim in the Cussy-dell, by the following observation which, on these occasions, he invariably made :—" Ah ! I saw Old N—k grinning on the ivied rock as I dragged such-a-one along the dell !" Marshall survived the plague a many years.

The last day of August, the sixth and twenty-

sixth, were the only days during that awful month
on which none died : while the whole number who
perished in the other twenty-eight days was seventy-
eight. This number of deaths must be considered
really appalling, especially when it is taken into
estimation that the population of the village on the
first of August was considerably under two hundred. The havoc in this month was dreadful beyond all description. The houses from the eastern
end to the middle of the village were now nearly
all empty. An awful gloom pervaded this part;
broken, however, at times by the sudden shriek
of one whom the blood-scented pest discovered in
some lone and secluded corner. The inhabitants
of the extreme western part of the village, who
were at that time very few, shut themselves close
up in their houses; nor would they on any occasion whatever, cross a small rivulet eastward, which
runs under the street in that part of Eyam. That
portion of the street which crosses this small stream
is called at this day " Fiddlers-Bridge ;" and it is
very commonly asserted, that the plague never
crossed it westward. This, I think, is hardly correct; but as there were but very few inhabitants
in that direction, the plague could not make any
great devastation. Indeed, as we shall see hereafter,
those who fled at the breaking out of the disease,
were principally, if not exclusively, inhabitants of
that part, and consequently, there would be but
very few left. One man, however, in the upper
or western part of the village, is said to have taken
the distemper and died by intending to visit a sister
who was a widow, and who dwelt in the Lydgate,
or the eastern part of Eyam. It is told, that this
man heard by chance, late one evening, in the latter end of August, that his sister, for whom he had

the greatest affection, was taken ill of the plague.
Being much troubled, he came to the determination of visiting her, even at the sacrifice of life.
Early next morning, he arose, unknown to his
family, and proceeded down the silent street to her
abode.   The door opened at his touch, but all was
still, he hastened to her bed, but it was empty and
stripped.   No enquiry of the fate of his sister was
requisite; she had died the preceding night, and
Marshall Howe had consigned her to a grave in
an adjoining garden, and had rifled her dwelling
long before the break of day.   The man returned
to his family full of grief and sorrow; but, he went
not alone—the invisible pest accompanied him, and
swept him and all his family into their graves, in
the short space of a few days.   Thus, like leaves
in Autumn, fell the villagers of Eyam, in the terrible and fatal month of August, 1666.

. September was unusually hot, and the plague
raged with unmitigated violence, considering the
amount of population left.   Almost every day in
this month had its victim; and the few that were
left, were now become so familiar with death, that
the announcement of the dissolution of any no
longer excited scarcely any notice whatever.   A
dreamy stillness reigned around the nearly desolated
village; it was canopied by a dark and deepening
gloom, which fancy might imagine had been formed
by the incessant accumulation of sorrowful respira-
tions.   The last day of September was one of the
few days during that month unattended by the
death of a victim.   Although the inhabitants at the
beginning of September were reduced to a very
few, still the insatiated pest carried away twenty-
four during that month.   October came, the month
in which it ceased; yet, up to the eleventh, it still

carried on the work of destruction, with but little relaxation of fury. On the eleventh of October, 1666, this awful minister of death, after having from the first day of the same month, destroyed fifteen out of about forty-five, totally ceased. After having swept away five-sixths of the inhabitants of Eyam, this the greatest enemy of the human race, was exhausted with excessive slaughter, and in the last conflict, worsted and destroyed and buried with the last victim.

Of the number who perished at Eyam by the hand of this direful plague, there are different accounts. The Register, which is undoubtedly as correct as can be expected from the confusion of the time, states the number of victims to be 259 ; while there is another account as follows :—" 259 of ripe age, and 58 children."[*] But as the number mentioned in the Register contains children, the latter account is most probably incorrect. This devastation is certainly appalling, when the amount of population at the commencement of the calamity is considered, which amount has generally been stated at 330. From the number of families visited by the plague, mentioned in the subsequent letter of Mompesson, it would, I opine, be nearer the mark, to say 350, or perhaps a few more. The number of deaths taken from the latter amount would leave 91. But a many fled at the first appearance of the distemper; some of whom never returned. Bradshaws, the then most wealthy family in the village, left it with precipitation, and never came back. A family of the name of Furness, took refuge at Farnsley, or Foundley, a farmhouse, about a mile from Eyam. Mr. Richard

* De Spiritualibus Pecci.

Furness, the poet, a native of Eyam, and the present schoolmaster of Dore, near Sheffield, is a
lineal descendant of that family. A man of the
name of Merril, who lived at the Hollins-House,
Eyam, built a hut on Eyam Moor, and resided
therein until the plague abated. A hut was built
a little beyond Riley by a family named Cotes,
who dwelt there during that terrible time. The
little dale that runs up to Foundley was nearly full
of huts, built under the projecting rocks. There
were others in the Cussy dell; and on various
parts of the Moor the remains of these fugitive
residences have existed, till very lately. Mompesson's children, as we have seen, were sent away,
and many others undoubtedly, who would not return for some time after the plague. Hence we may
conclude, that there would be but very few left of
those who tarried within the precincts of the village; in fact, it is a very current tradition that,
two dozen funeral cakes, were, for some years subsequent to the plague, sufficient for the whole
village, inclusive of the few distant relatives of the
deceased. And I may here add, that of all the
desolating traces of that destructive malady, there
is none which to the present day has been more
generally talked of, than that the main street, from
one end of the village to the other, was grown over
with grass; and, it is said, that kingcups and other
flowers grew in the very middle of the road. This,
however, one would imagine, could hardly be the
case in 1666; but more probably in 1667, and a
few succeeding years. That the village was almost
desolate there is no doubt; and in the following
sublime language of Ossian, it may be said:—
" There the thistle shook its lonely head : the moss

whistled to the wind. The fox looked out from the windows, the rank grass of the wall waved round its head."

The winter which succeeded the cessation of the pestilence was, by the very few who were left, wholly spent in burning the furniture of the pest houses, and likewise nearly all the bedding and clothing found in the village : reserving scarcely anything to cover their nakedness. The necessary articles of apparel were fumigated and purified ; and every means that could be suggested, were taken to prevent the resurrection of the horrid pest. But, the awful dread of this deadly monster ; the condition of the village at the termination of its ravages, will be best shown by giving, after the following letter of Mompesson's, a few very popular and authentic traditions of that unspeakable and agonizing time :—

" To John Beilby, Esq., ———, Yorkshire.
" Eyam, Nov. 20, 1666.

" DEAR SIR,—I suppose this letter will seem to you no less than a miracle, that my habitation is *inter vivos.* I have got these lines transcribed by a friend, being loth to affright you with a letter from my hands. You are sensible of my state, the loss of the kindest wife in the world, whose life was amiable and end most comfortable. She was in an excellent posture when death came, which fills me with assurances that she is now invested with a crown of righteousness. I find this maxim verified by too sad experience: *Bonum magis carendo quam fruendo cernitur.* Had I been as thankful as my condition did deserve, I might have had my dearest dear in my bosom. But now farewell all happy days, and God grant I may repent my sad ingratitude !

" The condition of the place has been so sad, that I persuade myself *it did exceed all history and example.* Our town has become a Golgotha, the place of a skull; and had there not been a small remnant, we had been as Sodom, and like to Gomorrah. My ears never heard such doleful lamentations—my nose never smelled such horrid smells, and my eyes never beheld such ghastly spectacles. Here have been 76 families visited within my parish, out of which 259 persons died. Now (blessed be

God) all our fears are over, for none have died of the plague
since the eleventh of October, and the pest houses have been
long empty. I intend (God willing) to spend this week in seeing all woollen clothes fumed and purified, as well for the satisfaction as for the safety of the country. Here have been such
burning of goods that the like, I think, was never known. For
my part, I have scarcely apparel to shelter my body, having
wasted more than I needed merely for example. During this
dreadful visitation, I have not had the least symptom of disease,
nor had I ever better health. My man had the distemper, and
upon the appearance of a tumour I gave him some chemical antidotes, which operated, and after the rising broke, he was very
well. My maid continued in health, which was a blessing; for
had she quailed, I should have been ill set to have washed and
gotten my provisions. I know I have had your prayers; and I
conclude that the prayers of good people have rescued me from
the jaws of death. Certainly I had been in the dust, had not
Omnipotence itself been conquered by holy violence.

" I have largely tasted the goodness of the Creator, and the
grim looks of death did never yet affright me. I always had a
firm faith that my babes would do well, which made me willing
to shake hands with the unkind, froward world; yet I shall
esteem it a mercy if I am frustrated in the hopes I had of a translation to a better place, and God grant that with patience I may
wait for my change, and that I may make a right use of His
mercies : as the one hath been tart, so the other hath been sweet
and comfortable.

" I perceive by a letter from Mr Newby, of your concern for
my welfare. I make no question but I have your unfeigned love
and affection. I assure you, that during my troubles you have
had a great deal of room in my thoughts. Be pleased, dear Sir,
to accept of the presentments of my kind respects, and impart
them to your good wife, and all my dear relations. I can assure
you that a line from your hand will be welcome to your sorrowful and affectionate nephew,

                              " WILLIAM MOMPESSON."

Thus wrote this affectionate spirit—thus he describes the sufferings of his flock, which sufferings,
however, will be further and more fully detailed in
the following traditions of this terrible calamity:—

When the plague broke out with such tremen-
dous violence in the latter end of the summer of
1665, there lived in a humble straw-thatched cottage, a little west of the church, a very happy and

contented family, named Sydall: consisting of husband, wife, five daughters, and one son. The father, son, and four daughters, took the infection and died in the space of twenty-five days, in October, 1665; leaving the hapless mother and one daughter. The mother had now nothing to render her disconsolate case bearable but her only surviving daughter Emmot; a very modest and handsome village maid. Emmot had for some time, with her mother's approbation, received the fervent addresses of a youth named Rowland, who resided in Middleton Dale, about a mile south-east of Eyam. He had daily visited her and sympathized with her on the death of her father, brother, and four young sisters. Often and anxiously had she remonstrated with him on the danger of his visits; but nothing could deter him from nightly pacing the devoted village, until the death-breathing pest threatened total desolation to the surrounding country, if intercourse were allowed. The happy scene when Rowland and Emmot were to cast their lots together, had been appointed to take place at the ensuing wakes; and fervently did they pray that the pestilence would cease. The ring, the emblem of endless and unchanging love, had been presented by Rowland to his beloved Emmot; and by her it was treasured as the certain pledge of the fidelity of his love,—of the sincerity of his affection. Frequently would she retire into her chamber, and bring it forth from its sanctuary and place it on her finger; while her eyes sparkled with meaning,—while through those bright portals of her mind, came forth her thoughts in language more eloquent than words. Rowland was seen each morn hasting along the dale to his occupation. Lightsome were his steps; his whistling echoed from rock to rock : and his soul glowed with all the charms of anticipated bliss. Thus this loving pair indulged in dreaming of future happiness ; thus they cherished the fond hope of connubial joy, on the very eve of separation !

Towards the latter end of April, 1666, the lovely Emmot was seized by the terrific pest, and hurried to her grave on the thirtieth of the same month. Rowland heard a brief rumour of the dreadful tidings and his hopes were scattered. The brand of general abhorrence with which he would be marked if he, at that period of the pestilence, attempted to venture into the deathful village, debarred him from ascertaining the fate of his Emmot. Often, however, would his love and dreadful anxiety urge him to cross the fearful bound—the horrible circle of death. But, to bring the pestilence home to his own family; to incur the everlasting infamy of spreading so terrible a disease, with the almost certainty of death on his own part, happily deterred him, on each attempt, from entering the poisonous " Upas vale."

On one occasion, however, Rowland ascended a hill contiguous to Eyam; and thence he looked over the silent village for hours. It was Sabbath eve,

> " But yet no Sabbath sound
> Came from the village ;—no rejoicing bells
> Were heard; no groups of strolling youths were found,
> Nor lovers loitering on the distant fells.
> No laugh, no shout of infancy, which tells
> Where radiant health and happiness repair ;
> But silence, such as with the lifeless dwells
> Fell on his shuddering heart and fixed him there,
> Frozen with dreams of death and bodings of despair."
> WILLIAM AND MARY HOWITT.

It was some time after the plague had ceased that Rowland summoned up sufficient courage to

enter the village, and to learn the fate of his Emmot. Glimmering hope and fearful apprehension
alternately possessed his mind, as his faltering
steps brought him to the verge of the village. He
stood on a little eminence at the eastern entrance
of the place, and glanced for a few moments
around; but he saw no smoke ascend from the
ivy-adorned chimnies — nothing but the sighing
breeze broke the still expanse, and he felt chained
to the spot by terror and dismay. At length he
ventured into the silent village, but he suddenly
stopped, looking as much aghast as if he had seen
the portentous inscription which met the eye of
Dante when the shade of Virgil led him to the
porch of Erebus. He then passed slowly on, gazing intensely on the desolate blank. A noiseless
gloom pervaded the lonely street; no human form
appeared; no sound of life was heard; and Rowland exclaimed, " O ! once happy village ! thou
art now a ruin, such as a mighty tempest leaves
when it has swept away the beauties of a garden !"
Filled with unspeakable amazement he looked on
each silent cottage; a hollow stillness reigned
therein, and,

" Horror round
Waved her triumphant wings o'er the untrodden ground."
WILLIAM AND MARY HOWITT.

Then towards the cot of his Emmot he bent his
way. His direful forebodings increased with every
step. As he approached the dwelling his heart
swelled and beat with painful emotion; but ere he
reached the place a solitary boy appeared and
thus the sorrowful tidings told :—" Ah ! Rowland,
thy Emmot's dead and buried in the Cussy Dell !"
This sudden disclosure struck Rowland with unutterable grief; he clung to an adjoining wall, and

H

there stood awhile combating with feelings keen
and unspeakable. At the death of Emmot, her
mother, frantic with despair, fled to the Cussy
Dell, and there dwelt with some fugitive relatives.
Rowland, after some time, proceeded to take a last
farewell of the abode of his Emmot; the once
happy place where he had spent so many happy
hours. He reached the threshold, over which the
grass grew profusely; the half-open door yielded
to his hand, and he entered the silent dwelling
filled with unimaginable sensations. On the hearth
and floor the grass grew up from every chink; the
tables and chairs in their usual places stood: the
pewter plates and pans with rust were flecked;
and the once sweet warbling linnet in its cage was
dead. Rowland wept as he left the tenantless
dwelling; his dreadful apprehensions were verified;
and until death closed his eyes at a very old age,
he frequently dropped a tear to the memory of his
once lovely Emmot.

A young woman was married from Eyam to
Corbor, about two miles distant, just before the
breaking out of the plague. She left a mother in
Eyam, who dwelt in a cottage alone, in great indi-
gence. When the plague was making the greatest
carnage, the old woman took the infection, and
her daughter, unknown to her husband, came to
see her, not knowing, however, that she was ill.
Great was her consternation at finding her poor
old mother writhing in dreadful agonies. She returned to Corbor the same day, very much terrified at the horrid scenes she had witnessed in the
village. On the succeeding night she was taken
very ill, and her husband and neighbours became
almost frantic with fear lest she should have
brought the distemper from Eyam. The follow-

ing day she was a very deal worse, and before
night all the terrific symptoms of the pest became
manifest, and she expired in great pain on the
second day of her illness. The village of Corbor
was alarmed beyond description; but, strange to
say, no one else took the infection.*

Some few, in Eyam, who had the plague, recovered; and the first was a Margaret Blackwell.
The tradition says that she was about sixteen or
eighteen years of age when she took the distemper;
and that her father and whole family were dead,
excepting one brother, at the time of her sickness.
Her brother was one morning obliged to go to the
coalpit; and he arose very early, cooked himself
some bacon, and started, being certain, as he said,
that he should find his sister dead when he came
back. Margaret, almost dying with excessive
thirst, got out of bed for something to drink; and
finding a small wooden piggin with something in
which she thought was water, but which was the
fat from the bacon which her brother had just
cooked, she drank it all off, returned to bed again,
and found herself soon after rather better. She,
however, had not the least hope of surviving :—

"But nature rallied, and her flame still burn'd—
Sunk in the socket, glimmer'd and return'd;
The golden bowl and silver cord were sound;
The cistern's wheel revolved its steady round;
Fire—vital fire—evolved the living steam,
And life's fine engine pump'd the purple stream."
                                        FURNESS.

On her brother's return he found her, to his
great surprise, a very deal better; she eventually

* There was a very bad fever (some say it was the plague) in
Corbor in 1632, when a many died. There are some grave-
stones in the vicinity with the initials J. C. A. C. and several
others, dated 1632. These initials are supposed to relate to a
family of the name of Cook.

recovered, and lived to a good old age. Drinking adventitiously the contents of the wooden piggin, has generally been considered the cause of her unexpected resuscitation.

Towards the latter end of the summer of the dreadful pest, a man of the name of Merril, of the Hollins-house, Eyam, erected, as I have before noticed, a hut near the summit of Sir William, wherein he dwelt to escape the plague, having only a cock with him, which he had taken for a companion. In this solitary retreat they lived together for about a month, with nothing to cheer them but the wild bee wandering with merry song. Merril would frequently, during this solitary sojourn, descend to a point of the hill from which he could glance over the fated place; but nothing could he perceive in the distance but the direful havoc of the awful scourge, as exhibited in the increasing graves in the fields of the village. One morning, however, his companion the cock, strutted from a corner of the hut into the heath, and after glancing about, sprang from the ground with flapping wings, nor stopped in its airy course until it arrived at its former residence, Hollins-house. Merril pondered a day or two over the meaning of his companion's abrupt desertion, and at last he thus soliloquized:—" Noah knew when the dove went forth and returned not again that the waters had subsided, and that the face of the earth was dry." He, therefore, took up his altitudes and returned to his former residence, where he found his cock. The plague had abated, and Merril and his cock lived many years together at the Hollins-house, after the pestilence was totally extinguished.

The helpless condition of the inhabitants of Eyam, in that dreadful season, may be seen from the following fact:—

A little west of Eyam, there resided, at a house called Shepherd's Hall, or Shepherd's Flat, a family of the name of Mortin, who suffered greatly during the plague. This family consisted of husband, wife, and one child; the wife being, however, when the plague broke out so fiercely in 1666, in an advanced state of pregnancy. There was another house very near to Mortin's, inhabited by a widow woman and some children, named Kempe; and the children of this woman had brought the infection to the Shepherd's Flat, by playing with the children of Eyam. When the time of Mortin's wife's pregnancy was expired no one would come near to assist on the occasion of giving birth to her child. She was very ill, and declared that without assistance she should die. Mortin, in the last extremity of despair, was compelled to assist in the act of parturition. The eldest child he had during the time shut up in a room, where it screamed and called out "daddy" and "mammy" incessantly, being almost petrified with fear. Very soon after, both children and mother took the distemper and died, and Mortin buried them successively with his own hands at the end of his habitation. The other family of Kempes all died, and Mortin was left the only human being at Shepherd's Flat, where he lived in solitude for some years after the plague. A greyhound and four cows were his companions; one of the cows he milked to keep the greyhound and himself. To such an extent did this horrible pest carry on human desolation, that hares, rabbits, and other kinds of game multiplied and overran the vicinity of Eyam; Mortin's greyhound could have gone out and brought in a hare in a few minutes, at any time of the day.

That the surrounding country was greatly alarmed at the devastation of the pest at Eyam, the following accounts are sufficient evidence :—

At the period of this dreadful malady, Tideswell, west of Eyam about five miles, was one of the principal market-towns in the Peak; and it was frequented on the market-days by great numbers from the wide-scattered villages. The consternation into which those who regularly attended, as well as the inhabitants of the place, were thrown, by the appalling reports of the pestilence at Eyam, caused a watch to be appointed at the eastern entrance of Tideswell, to question all who came that way, and to prevent any one from Eyam from passing on any business whatever. A woman who dwelt in that part of Eyam called Orchard Bank, was, during the greatest carnage of the pest, compelled by some pressing exigency to go to the market at Tideswell; knowing, however, that it would be impossible to pass the watch if she told whence she came; she therefore had recourse to the following stratagem. The watch, on her arrival, thus authoritatively addressed her :—" Whence comest thou ?" " From Orchard Bank," she replied. " And where is that ?" the watch asked again; " Why, verily," said the woman, " it is in the land of the living." The watch, not knowing the place, suffered her to pass; but she had scarcely reached the market when some person knew her, and whence she came. " The plague ! the plague ! a woman from Eyam ! the plague ! a woman from Eyam !" immediately resounded from all sides; and the poor creature terrified almost to death, fled as fast as she possibly could. The infuriated multitude chased her at a distance, for near a mile out of the market-place; and pelted her with volleys of stones, mud, sods, and other missiles. She returned to Orchard Bank, bruised and otherwise worse for her daring prevarication. The dread of this infectious disease, as manifested in the case of this woman, and in the institution of keeping watch in the approximate villages, is no ways marvellous; for, in the accounts of the constables of Sheffield, there is the following item :—" Charges about keeping people from Fullwood Spring (ten miles from Eyam) at the time the plague was at Eam." Fuel was an article which the inhabitants had to encounter great difficulties in obtaining; those who fetched it from the coal-pits had to make circuitous routes, and represent themselves as coming from other places. One man on this journey unthinkingly let it slip that he came from Eyam, on which he was greatly abused and driven back, with his horses unladen. In a will of a Mr. Rowland Mower, Eyam, made when the plague was at its greatest height, there is, as near as can be recollected, the following allusion to the almost certainty of death of the whole population :—" Inasmuch as a great calamity has befallen the town, or village of Eyam; as death has already entered my dwelling; as all are in daily expectation of death; and as I humbly consider myself on the verge of eternity, I therefore, while in sound mind, thus give and bequeath, as hereafter noted, my worldly effects."

The dreadful panic which the inhabitants of the neighbouring villages experienced, by any one venturing therefrom to Eyam, may be sufficiently seen by the following singular and well authenticated fact :—

During the plague, a man who lived at Bubnel, near Chatsworth, named ———, an ancestor of

Mr. W. Howard, Barlow, had either to come to
Eyam, or pass through Eyam, with a load of wood,
which he was in the habit of carrying from the
woods at Chatsworth, to the surrounding villages.
His neighbours fervently remonstrated with him
before his departure, on the impropriety and danger
of going near Eyam; being, however, a fine, robust
man, he disregarded their admonitions, and proceeded to Eyam with the wood. The day turned
out very wet and boisterous; and as no one would
accompany him to assist in unloading the wood,
great delay was thereby occasioned. A severe
cold was the result, and shortly after his arrival at
home, he was attacked with a slight fever. The
neighbours became exceedingly alarmed at his indisposition; they naturally concluded that he had
taken the infection; and they were so incensed at
his daring and dangerous conduct, that they
threatened to shoot him if he attempted to leave
his house. A man was appointed to watch and
give the alarm if he crossed his own threshold.
The consternation of the inhabitants of Bubnel
and neighbouring places, excited the notice of the
Earl of Devonshire, who had, either at his own
request or otherwise, the particulars of the case
laid before him. The Noble Earl, being anxious
that no unnecessary alarm should be excited, rea-
soned with the persons who waited on him from
Bubnel, on the impropriety of rashly judging because the man was ill, it was necessarily the plague.
He told them to go back, and he would send his
Doctor the next day at a certain hour to examine
into the nature of the man's illness. The interview,
either at the suggestion of the Earl, or from the
Doctor's fear, was appointed to take place across
the river Derwent, which flows close by Bubnel.

At the appointed time, the Doctor took his station
on the eastern side of the river, where it makes a
bend, which, on this and other accounts, made the
distance to the sick man's appointed station greater.
A sentinel informed the man of the arrangement,
and he descended, well wrapped up, to the western
side of the river. The affrighted neighbours looked
on from a distance, while the Doctor interrogated
the sick man at great length. The Doctor at last
pronounced him free from the disorder; prescribed
him some medicine; and the man, who was then
much better, soon recovered.*

Mompesson left Eyam in 1669, three years after
the plague; but the horrors which it had dissemi-
nated, had extended even to Eakring in Notting-
hamshire, and to the time of his leaving Eyam for
the living of that place. This benefice was presented to him by his friend and patron, Sir George
Saville. On his going to take possession of the
living of Eakring, the inhabitants refused admit-
ting him into the village; in consequence of their
terrors of "the cloud and whirlwind of death," in
which he had walked. A little house or hut was
therefore erected for him in Rufford Park, where
he resided in seclusion until their fears died away.
Such was the horror of that desolating infection;
such was the dreadful impressions which it created
even in far more distant places. Having now given,
very imperfectly indeed, a few of the traditions of
this awful time, I shall proceed to commit to paper
the details of the rapid extinction of the Talbots
and Hancocks, of Riley: two families who were
carried off by the plague with horrid dispatch; and
whose brief transition from health to sickness, from

* The Doctor's prescription is now in the hands of Dr.
Nicholson, son-in-law of Mr. W. Howard, Barlow.

sickness to death, was attended with circumstances never before experienced.

> " O ! reader ! reader ! had we been
> Spectators of the real scene."   S. T. HALL.

Riley Graves are about a quarter of a mile eastward of Eyam, on the top, or rather on the slope of a hill, the base of which partially terminates in Eyam. These mountain *tumuli* are generally known to be the burial places of the Hancock family during the plague. Perhaps there is no place capable of producing such peculiar and serious impressions; such sedate, venerable, and unspeakable sensations. These insulated memorials of the hapless sufferers, viewed with the surrounding scenery, give a tone to the feelings as pathetic as inexpressible. All the lighter emotions of the heart are chained down in prostrate abeyance: we feel as if we were holding communion with the spirits who murmur a saddening requiem to pleasure and frolicsome gaiety. All seems so hallowed: so over-shadowed, and so deeply imbued with solemnity. Were I competent to describe the impressive scenery of Riley Graves, it would be only a work of supererogation; seeing that it has already received the deeply impassioned strokes and the heart-softening touches of the elegant authors of " Peak Scenery," and " Rambles in Derbyshire :" therefore I shall proceed to give the details of the almost total extinction of the family of Hancock, and the sole extinction of that of Talbot—the two families who resided at Riley at the commencement of the desolation of Eyam; with a particular notice of the places of their interment; and (as is indispensably necessary in this work) a brief description of the surrounding scenery.

Those who have visited Riley Grave Stones

have unavoidably noticed, about fifty yards from
the enclosed cemetery, a small ash tree, it stands
in a north-east direction of the stones, and it was
a few yards south of this tree where stood the habitation of the Hancocks. There is not the least
remains of that dwelling to be seen at this day;
the disconsolate mother, after burying her husband
and six children, as hereafter described, deserted
it; and it was sometime after carried away to re-
pair the neighbouring fences. The house in which
the Talbots lived was about two hundred and fifty
yards west or rather north-west of that of Hancocks; the present Riley-farm house is built on
its site. The Manchester road to Sheffield passed,
in those days, close by this house, and Talbots,
being blacksmiths, had a smithy adjoining the
house, and close to the road. Besides this occupation, they farmed part of Riley old land, and
Hancocks the other. The Talbot family consisted of Richard, his wife, three sons, and three
daughters: one son, however, had left Riley, and
lived at some distance, before the commencement
of the plague, in his own family, and therefore escaped. The high and airy situation of Riley, one
would imagine, ought to have operated against the
distemper; and being besides a full quarter of a
mile from Eyam, the two families were not compelled to have any communication with the inhabitants thereof. How or by what means this subtle
agent of death, found the way to Riley, is not now
known; most probably some of the Talbot family
brought it from Eyam, as they all perished before
the infection, or at least before the death of any
one of the Hancocks. The pestilence had raged
full ten months in Eyam, before the Talbots of
Riley were visited by this deathful messenger.

On the fifth of July, 1666, died Briget and Mary, daughters of Richard and Catherine Talbot, of Riley. They were young and beautiful : they had sported with innocence and mirth on the flowery heath only a few days before death came and laid his cold, chilly hand on their lovely bosoms. Often had they roved on the neighbouring moors, with hearts swelling with joy, and pure as the snow of their mountains : ah! they had spent full many a sunny day, in chasing the many-hued butterfly, amidst the busy hum of the wild and toilsome bees; and then, like two sweet roses just bursting into bloom, they were suddenly plucked from their lonely, parent bed. Thus these two lovely girls fell victims to the horrid pest ; thus they reluctantly stooped beneath death's fearful arch in one sad, direful day. Their weeping and terrified father immediately committed them to the earth beside his mournful home. On the seventh of the same month, he performed the same awful task on Ann, another of his hapless daughters ; and on the eighteenth, on his wife Catherine. Robert, his son, died, and was buried on the twenty-fourth, and on the ensuing day, the father himself died and was buried, leaving one son, who on the thirtieth died also, and was buried, probably by the Hancocks, on the same day. Thus, from the fifth to the thirtieth of July, perished the whole of the household of the fated Talbots of Riley. They were interred nearly together, close by their habitation ; and in the orchard of the present Riley-house, a dilapidated tabular monument, with the following very nearly erased inscription, records their memories :—" Richard Talbot, Catherine his wife, 2 sons, and 3 daughters, buried July, 1666."

The pest now passed on to the habitation of the
Hancocks, where the work of death commenced
by the infection of John and Elizabeth, son and
daughter of John and Elizabeth Hancock. On
the third of August, only three days from the
death of the last of the Talbots, they both died,
and were buried at a little distance from their cottage, by the hands of their distracted mother. Although her husband and two other sons survived
four days after the first victims, yet tradition insists that the mother of this family buried them
herself, altogether unassisted. John, her husband,
and two sons, William and Oner, now sickened of this
virulent malady. She became frantic; she saw
that the whole family were destined to the same
fate as the Talbots, and she wrung her hands in
bitter despair. In the night of the sixth, Oner
died, and her husband a few minutes after, and
before morning, William gave his last struggling
gasp. Can imagination conceive anything so appalling as the case of this suffering woman : on
the third she buried a son and daughter, and in
the night of the following sixth, she closed the
eyes of her husband and two other sons. How
awful her situation; being far from any other
dwelling; not a soul to cheer her sinking spirits;
not a being to cast her sorrowing eyes upon, save
her two surviving children, whose lamentations
were carried afar on the startled morning breeze.
Such was the terrible night of the sixth of August,
to this woful woman; often she ran to the door
and called out in agony for help; then turning in
again she fell on her knees, and

" With hands to heaven out-spread,
Her frequent, fervent, orisons she said,
In loud response her childrens' voices rise,
And midnight's echo to their prayer replies."
LUCIEN BONAPARTE.

I

The beams of the following morning's sun fell on the shallow graves which she had made for her husband and two sons. Dreading to touch the putrid bodies, she, as she had done by the other, tied a towel to their feet, and dragged them on the ground in succession to their graves. Hapless woman, surely no greater woe, ever crushed a female heart.

The end of two short days, from the seventh to the ninth, saw her again digging another grave amongst the blooming heath for her daughter Alice. On the morning of the next day, the tenth, Ann, her only child left at home, sunk and breathed her last. Thus

> " each morn that rose,
> Her *grief* redoubled, and renewed her woes."
>
> LUCIEN BONAPARTE.

She consigned her to a grave beside her brothers and sisters; weeping in tears of sorrow until the fountains of grief became as dry as the sands of the desert. A few days after the death of her last child, she left her habitation at Riley, and went to an only son who had been, some years before the plague, bound an apprentice in Alsop-fields, Sheffield; with whom she spent the remainder of her sorrowful days. It was this son who erected the tomb and stones to the awful memory of his fated family; and it was one of his descendants, a Mr. Joseph Hancock, who, about the year 1750, discovered, " or rather recovered," in Sheffield, the art of plating goods.*

The houses in the top part of Stoney Middleton are nearly on a level with Riley-Graves; divided by two dells or narrow dales. The inhabitants of these houses, according to a very popular tradition, watched with profound awe the mother of the

* Vide Rhodes' Peak Scenery.

Hancocks, morning after morning digging the graves for her husband and children; and dragging them on the ground from their dwelling, and burying them therein. Awful and terrible scene. Did they not in imagination hear her audibly exclaim with the holy prophet? " Oh! that my head were waters, and mine eyes a fountain of tears, that I might weep day and night."

It has been observed by some writers that Riley, or Riley-graves, was the general burial place of the victims of the plague; this is, however, a mistake: none was buried there but the Talbots and Hancocks. The Talbots I have never seen noticed by any writer. Six head-stones and a tabular tomb record the memories of the Hancocks. The site of the graves was originally on the common or moor, on the verge of which was the dwelling of the Hancocks. That part of the common was afterwards inclosed, and the stones, which lay horizontally and marked precisely the places of the graves, were placed in an upright position, and somewhat nearer together. Thomas Birds, Esq., Eyam, an highly inestimable character, and profound antiquarian, caused these memorials to be put in a better state of preservation. He purchased the ground whereon they lay; but, since his death, or just before, it became the property of Thomas Burgoine, Esq., of Edenzor, who for the better security of those relics of the plague, has removed them still nearer each other, and erected a wall round them in the form of a heart. It is hoped that the owner will prevent any further change in the situation of these sacred stones. On the top of the tomb there is the following inscription and quaint rhymes :—

" John Hancock, sen., Buried August 7, 1666.

Remember man
As thou goest by,
As thou art now,
Even once was I;
As I doe now
So must thou lie,
Remember man
That thou must die."

On the four sides of the tomb are the words—
Horam, Nescitis, Orate, Vigilate. On the head-
stones the inscriptions are as follows :—

Elizabeth Hancock, Buried Aug. 3, 1666.
John Hancock, Buried Aug. 3, 1666.
Oner Hancock, Buried Aug. 7, 1666.
William Hancock. Buried Aug. 7, 1666.
Alice Hancock, Buried Aug. 9, 1666.
Ann Hancock, Buried Aug. 10, 1666.

It is impossible for the tourist to describe his
feelings fully and minutely when he visits this hallowed and lonely place; he beholds, in the language of Ossian, " green tombs with their rank
whistling grass; with their stones of mossy heads;"
and his soul becomes suddenly overcharged with
grave and solemn emotions. The scenery around
these rude and simple monuments of eventful mortality, is highly picturesque; and adds greatly to
the impressiveness of the sensations which a visit
to this place invariably creates. Standing within
this paling we behold to the left a long range of
sable rocks sheltering the ancient villages of Corbor and Calver. Farther on, Chatsworth meets
our view, and forms a conspicuous object in the
prospect. This costly mansion, surrounded by
such wide contrasting objects, has an unique effect:
it has a magic-like appearance. Proud Masson is
seen in the dim distance holding imperial sway
over a thousand lesser hills. To the right we
glance on the plain tower of Eyam church rising
above the ivy-adorned cottages in rural magnificence. Lovely village, amidst thy dells we hear

the muses of thy living and departed minstrels in
sweet communion sing. Still farther on we see
the peaks of endless hills, where the winding,
classic Cressbrook flows,—the minstrel Newton's
Arethuse. And behind, plantations of young trees
are richly commingled with purple-blooming hea-
ther. Such are a few of the most prominent objects viewed from Riley-graves—" The Mountain
Tumuli," where heath-bells bloom—where nestling fern and rank grass grow—where lone and
still,

" Their green and dewy graves, the unconscious sufferers fill."
WILLIAM AND MARY HOWITT.

One hundred and seventy-six years have now
transpired since this unequalled and dreadful visitation ; and, therefore, many of the stones which
told of the calamities of Eyam, have been destroyed. In order that the future inhabitants of
Eyam may be enabled to point out to the tourist
most of the places where the ashes of the sufferers
repose, I shall describe in a few following pages
all the places where stones have been known to
exist; where bones and bodies have been found;
and where the still existing few memorials may be
seen.

In the Cossy-dell there were, about fifty years
ago, two or three grave-stones to the memory of a
portion, or the whole, of a family of the name of
Ragge; and the Register mentions four persons of
that name who died of the plague. These stones
have either been broken or carried away. It was
the last of these memorials which is the theme of
the short and beautiful poem, entitled " The Tomb
of the Valley;" written a few years ago by Richard
Furness.

At the Shepherds-Flat some stones existed until

very lately, to the memories of the Mortins and Kempes; two families who perished by the plague, with the solitary exception, as we have before seen, of one individual. These memorials, after having marked for more than a century and a half, the precise places where the mortal remains of the sufferers of Shepherds-Flat were deposited, have been destroyed by some late barbarian occupants of that secluded place. Bretton, about a mile north of Eyam, was visited by the plague; and a many grave-stones once recorded the names of those who died. A few still remain. The victims were of the families of Mortin, Hall, and Townsend. One of these sufferers was buried in Bretton-Clough, and a round stone still covers the grave, but without any inscription. In Eyam-edge some grave-stones were once seen near to the house now belonging to Mr. I. Palfreyman; but they have disappeared long ago. Behind, or rather at the west-end of some dwellings, now recognised as the Poor-houses, one or two of these stones which are said to have recorded the deaths of some persons of the name of Whitely, have been of late demolished. In a field adjoining the back part of the house occupied by Mr. J. Rippon, Eyam, one of these " melancholy tablets of mortality" once existed. That part of Eyam called the Townend was, about eighty years ago, bestrewed with these calamitous memoranda. Some have served for the flooring of houses and barns; while others have been broken up for numerous purposes. The house and barn contiguous to the Miners' Arms Inn was built on a small plot of ground which contained the uncon-secrated graves of a whole family at least. The stones which commemorated the untimely fate of these sufferers were sacrilegiously broken when

the present building was erected. A piece of waste
land at the east end of the village, now forming a
part of Slinn's Croft, must, from the number of
monumental stones it once contained, have been
the general place of interment for a many families.
Some of these humble tablets were inscribed with
a single H; probably the initial of Heald: the
name of a family of whom a many perished. This
brief and simple inscription is, however, equally as
applicable to two other families of the names of
Halksworth and Hadfield, who might inter their
deceased members in this place. One of these
stones, still existing, is to the memory of a woman
of the name of Talbot; and others were commemorative of many other persons of various
names. These mournful memorials, with their
serious and impressive records, are now, with one
single exception, no longer seen. They have been
wantonly and unnecessarily destroyed; and, principally, (as I am informed,) by a man, from whose
pretension to classical attainments, something different might have been expected. A want of becoming veneration for the remains of those un-
paralleled sufferers; an utter absence of a due
sense of feeling, must ever be the degraded characteristics of that being who has lent a hand to
destroy those simple monuments of the greatest
moral heroes that ever honoured and dignified
mankind! The inhabitants of Eyam ought to have
vied with each other in the preservation of every
relic of the eventful fate of the victims of the
plague; the ground in which their ashes are laid,
ought to have been for ever undisturbed; and the
tablets which told the story of their calamities
guarded as much as possible, even from the de-
facing hand of time. Alas! alas! such has not

been the case : nearly all the humble stones which
were laid to perpetuate their memories have been
demolished.

> " Ah ! There no more
> The green graves of the pestilence are seen ;
> O'er them the plough hath pass'd ; and harvests wave,
> Where haste and horror flung th' infectious corse."
>   ELLIOTT.

The following are, however, the few stones that
still remain :—

Besides Mrs. Mompesson's tomb there is another
in the church-yard, but the inscription is now obliterated; yet I believe it was erected to the memory
of a person of the name of Rowland, who died of
the plague in 1666. The Register mentions
several of this name, who were carried off during
that awful time. In a field behind the church,
known as Blackwell's Edge-field, there are two
stones with the following inscriptions :—" Margaret
Teyler, 1656 ;" " Alies Teyler, 1666." According
to the Register, Margaret was buried July 14,
1666; and Alies was one of the last who perished
by the hand of the pest. Nearly the whole of this
family died of the distemper, although there is no
mention of any other on the present existing stones.
It appears, however, that the father, mother, and
children of this family, died at long intervals, considering the sweeping, sudden, and awful desolation.

In a field adjoining Froggatt's factory, there is
an old dilapidated tabular tomb, with H. M. inscribed on one end. These letters are the initials
of Humphrey Merril, who was buried there on the
9th of September, 1666. In the parson's field, in
the Lydgate, Eyam Townend, two gravestones are
laid nearly parallel to each other, containing the
following records :—" Here lye buried George

Darby, who dyed July 4th, 1666;" "Mary, the daughter of George Darby, dyed September 4th, 1666." The house in which this family dwelt is supposed to have been contiguous to their graves. There is a tradition that this lovely young maiden was extremely beautiful and engaging; that she was frequently seen in the adjoining flowery fields; that she was suddenly seized by the terrific pest while gathering flowers in the field of her father's sepulchre; and that she lingered only one short day before she was laid beneath the daisy-sods, beside her father's grave. How sudden the change. Homer's beautiful simile on the death of Euphorbus, may be applied with equal felicity to the fate of this hapless young maiden :—

" As the young olive, in some sylvan scene,
Crown'd by fresh fountains with eternal green,
Lifts the gay head, in snowy flowerets fair,
And plays and dances to the gentle air;
When lo! a whirlwind from high heav'n invades
The tender plant, and withers all its shades;
It lies uprooted from its genial bed,
A lovely ruin, now defaced and dead."

A stone in the possession of Mr. John Slinn, of the King's Arms Inn, Eyam, has the following inscription: " Briget Talbot, Ano. Dom. 1666." She was the wife of Robert Talbot, clerk, and was buried on the fifteenth of August, 1666. The stone was found in a small piece of ground, now forming, as aforementioned, part of Slinn's croft, and it is hoped that this memorial of the desolation of Eyam, will be preserved, which I am happy to state, there is no doubt. This Robert Talbot was in holy orders, but where he officiated, or whether he ever exercised the sacred functions or not, I am not able to affirm. The house in which he resided is known to this day as the Parson's house. These calamitous tablets, with those at Riley, are all that now bear testimony of the plague at Eyam. Many have been destroyed, and probably a many more are buried beneath the surface of the gardens and fields of the village.

Within the present generation several human skeletons and other remains of the victims of the plague have been discovered in various parts of the village. In making some alterations in some buildings opposite the school, about twenty years ago, three skulls and other bones were found. From the position of the skulls, the bodies appeared to have been laid side by side, very near each other, and what was most particularly observed was, that the teeth were extremely white and perfect. The jaws of all the skulls had the requisite number of teeth, which were most remarkably sound. On making the new road from the Dale to the Town-end, fifteen years ago, a human skeleton, lying at full length, was found in a garden. It measured nearly six feet, and the teeth, as in the above case, were equally perfect. The skeleton, on account of the stature, was supposed to be that of a young man, and the whiteness and soundness of the teeth, were most probably owing to his being at the time of death in the vigour of life. An old house, opposite the Church, was pulled down a few years ago, when a human skeleton was found under the parlour floor. Two or three grave-stones, which had in part paved the same room, were destroyed at the same time. A very many persons can recollect having seen the stones, but all have forgot the particular inscriptions. In an old house on the Cross, now occupied by J. Wilson, miller, some human bones were found in removing part of the kitchen floor. There was a grave-stone, if not

some part of a human skeleton, once found in a
field which is now called Phillip's sitch. In a cleft
of the rocks in the dale side, some bones were
found a many years since, by Mr. Samuel Hall,
Eyam. These bones were undoubtedly the remains of some person or persons deposited there at
the time of the plague. In the Dale, very near
the Hanging Fat, some bones have been dug up.
There is no doubt whatever, that the remains of
the plague's victims are scattered far and wide in
and around the village. By way of concluding
this doleful subject, it may be proper to notice a
few particulars respecting the still existing difference of opinion concerning the respective merits of
Mompesson and Stanley, in the happy influence
exercised over the villagers of Eyam, during their
awful calamity.

It is insisted by a few, that Stanley exerted himself in mitigating the sufferings of the inhabitants
of Eyam during the plague, to a far greater degree
than Mompesson; that he was the principal means
of preventing the contagion from spreading to the
neighbouring villages; that the fame of Mompesson has cast an undue shade over the lofty virtues
of his pious predecessor; and that, for this and
other reasons, the venerable and conscientious Stanley has not had justice done to his memory. Without wishing to detract anything from the merits of
Mompesson, I must confess that there are grounds
for suspecting that Stanley has not had that justice
done him which he so deservedly merited. It is
lamentable that such should have been the case;
yet I believe, although there is no particular clue
to the motives of the persons by whom his name
has been kept back, that it will scarcely admit of
doubt. The following extract from Bagshaw's

Spiritualibus Pecci, quoted by Calamy, in his Lives of the Nonconformists, sufficiently corroborates what is here advanced:—" When he (Stanley) could not serve his people publicly, he was helpful to them in private. Some persons yet alive will testifie how helpful he was to his people when the pestilence prevailed in Eyam, that he continued with em when, AS IT IS WRITTEN, 259 persons of ripe age and 58 children were cut off thereby. When some who might have been better employed moved the then Noble Earl of Devonshire, Lord Lieutenant, to remove him out of the town, I am told by the creditable that he said, ' It was more reasonable that the whole country should in more than words testifie their thankfulness to him, who, together with the care of the town, had taken such care AS NO ONE ELSE DID, to prevent the infection of the towns adjacent.' "* The well-known veracious character of the venerable Apostle of the Peak, gives to his testimony the weight of indubitable truth. And I may here add, that the memory of Stanley amongst the inhabitants of Eyam is, to the present day, greatly revered and deservedly cherished. By some he is invariably designated as, THE GREAT GOOD MAN. He died at Eyam in the year 1670, " satisfied to the last in the cause of Nonconformity." The house in which he lived was, until it was pulled down, called Stanley's house. Tradition gives to this honourable character all the glowing virtues of the MAN OF ROSS:

" And what! no monument, inscription, stone?
His race, his form, his name almost unknown."—POPE.

---

* The Author, notwithstanding his appeal to some written testimony, is certainly mistaken as to the number who died of the plague.

This highly exalted character of Stanley must not be supposed to detract in the least from that of the benevolent Mompesson. No; Mompesson's memory is richly worthy of all the admiration with which it has been honoured. The living of Eyam was presented to him on the death of Sherland Adams, in 1664; only one year before the first breaking out of the plague. From the following passage in his letter to his uncle, J. Beilby, Esq., ——, Yorkshire, he appears to have been dissatisfied with his situation at Eyam:—" Had I been so thankful as my situation did deserve, I might have had my dearest dear in my bosom—God grant that I may repent my sad ingratitude !"—He seems, however, to have known with Seneca, that " Virtue is that perfect good, which is the complement of a happy life ; the only immortal thing that belongs to mortality." His virtue was not contemplative, but active : and it must be remembered, that this divine property is never so glorious as when exhibited in extremities. What a sublime sentiment he gave to the world in the following words, in his letter to Sir George Saville :—" I am not desirous that they (his children) should be great, but good ;" and he then adds, " my next request is, that they may be brought up in the fear and admonition of the Lord." When he considered himself on the verge of eternity, he thus in the purest spirit of philanthropy addresses his patron :—" I desire, Sir, that you will make choice of a humble, pious man to succeed me in my parsonage ; and could I see your face before my departure hence, I would inform you in which manner I think he may live comfortably amongst his people, which would be some satisfaction to me before I die." In another

K

part he says : " Never do any thing upon which
you dare not first ask the blessing of God." Such
were the requisitions and holy admonitions of this
admirable minister of Christ.   His high sense of
duty was made strikingly manifest on the following
occasion. The Deanery of Lincoln was generously
offered him ; but he humbly declined accepting it
in favour of a friend, whom he sincerely esteemed :
Dr. Fuller, not the author of " The British
Worthies." How noble! how disinterested! was this
Christian-like act of friendship. He, however, in
addition to the Rectory of Eakring, accepted of
the Prebends of York and Southwell. He married
for his second wife Mrs. Nuby, relict of Charles
Nuby, Esq., who bore him two daughters. He
died at Eakring, the 7th of March, 1708, in the
70th year of his age.   A brass plate, with a Latin
inscription, marks the place in the Church at
Eakring where his ashes repose.

Of this man, Miss Seward thus emphatically
observes :—" His memory ought never to die ! it
should be immortal· as the spirit that made it
worthy to live."

And is it not gratifying to the villagers of Eyam,
to know that the place of their humble residence
has been honoured by the deeds of such a disinterested, benevolent, and exalted character as
Mompesson?   The conduct of this ever-to-be-ad-
mired man was a pure emanation from the heart
of a Christian in spirit and truth.   And while
France glories in the name of the good Bishop of
Marseilles, England shall exult in her transcendant
rival—Mompesson, the village pastor of Eyam !*

---

* It would be doubly gratifying, had there been some honourable mention of Stanley by Mompesson, in one or all of his
letters.

It is lamentable that so little is known of the descendants of this worthy and dignified character. In Miller's " History of Doncaster," his son, George Mompesson, is mentioned as witness to an indenture, connected with the establishment of a library, in 1736, at Doncaster church. This said George Mompesson was rector of Barnborough, Yorkshire; he married Alice, daughter of John Broomhead, schoolmaster of Laughten-en-le-Morthen. She is buried in Barnborough church; and a Latin inscription distinguishes her grave: she died on the 16th of October, 1716, aged 47 years. Another inscription records the death of John, the son of George and Alice Mompesson, rector of Hassingham; he died on the 2nd of January, 1722, aged 32 years. Few or no descendants of this family are now left.[*]

" In the summer of 1751," writes Miss Seward, " five cottagers were digging on the heathy mountain above Eyam, which was the place of graves after the church-yard became too narrow a repository. The men came to something which had the appearance of having once been linen. Conscious of their situation, they instantly buried it again. In a few days, they all sickened of a putrid fever, and three of the five died. The disorder was contagious, and proved mortal to numbers of the inhabitants. My father, who was the Canon of Lichfield, resided in that city with his family, at the period when the subtle, unextinguished, though much-abated power of the most dreadful of all diseases awakened from the dust, in which it had slumbered 91 years." After a most careful in-

---

[*] The name—*Mompesson*—is not English: and it is believed that the immediate ancestors of the worthy Rector of Eyam of that name, were foreigners.

quiry, I am almost certain that Miss Seward was mistaken; at least, as respects the date. That some linen or woollen cloth was dug up at Riley, some very old persons have some faint recollection; but it could not be in 1757, and have produced such effects as Miss Seward describes; as the mortality in that year was only ordinary. In the month of January, 1779, the weather was unusually warm; indeed, most remarkably so; and in the ensuing summer, a bad fever broke out, which carried off upwards of twenty of the stoutest persons in the village—chiefly men. This happened in the middle of the summer; and the flesh meat which the villagers had provided for the wakes, became tainted and green, in a most astonishing short time: so much so, that it was nearly all buried without being tasted. Those who died, swelled in the neck and groin; and the villagers apprehended that the terrible ghost of the plague had risen from the dust. This contagious fever after a while passed away. If it were not to this time that Miss Seward alludes, she was totally misinformed. In 1813, another fever made its appearance, and hurried a few to their graves, with great speed. ᛁ On both these occasions, the desolation of Eyam, in 1666, was the theme of the whole village. It is singular that, even to this day, the villagers express their disapprobation of one another in the following phrases:—" The plague on thee," and " The plague take thee."

In the year 1766, the Rev. Mr. Seward preached a centenary sermon in the church of Eyam, in commemoration of the plague. The sermon was written with great descriptive power: it drew forth abundant tears from the sobbing auditors. It is hoped that in the year 1866, a second centenary sermon will be preached at the same place and on the same event.

I shall take but little notice of the several causes which the few survivors believed had brought down the plague on the village as a judgment. At the wakes preceding the first appearance of the pest, some few wanton youths are said to have driven a young cow into the church during divine service; and to this profane act the dreadful visitation was by some ascribed. A persecuted Catholic, of the name of Garlick, who was taken prisoner at Padley Hall, in the reign of Elizabeth, is said to have been much abused as he passed through Eyam, in custody, when he said something which has been, by some, construed into a prediction of the plague. These with other presumed causes of the awful scourge must be considered fanciful. The great omniscient Disposer of events in his wisdom permitted it; and we poor worms of creation must not pretend to know for what wise end it was intended; nor must we more presumptuously presume

" To teach eternal wisdom how to rule."—POPE.

According to the Register, the following are the names of those who died of the plague, with the dates of their respective deaths. Their ages are not given. Some were young, as they are mentioned as being the children of such and such persons. I shall, for brevity's sake, only give the simple names :—

BURIED.	A.D.	BURIED.	A.D.
George Vicars, Sept. 7,	1665	Elizabeth Thorpe Oct. 1,	1665
Edward Cooper 22	...	Margret Bands 3	...
Peter Halksworth ...23	...	Mary Thorpe 3	...
Thomas Thorpe ...26	..	Sythe Torre 6	...
Sarah Sydall 30	...	William Thorpe ... 7	...
Mary Thorpe 30	...	Richard Sydall 11	...
Matthew Bands, Oct. 1	...	William Torre 13	...

K 2

BURIED.	A.D.	BURIED.	A.D.
Alice Torre (his wife) Oct. ...13, 1665		Jon. Thos. Willson, March —, 1666	
John Sydall 14	...	John Talbot .. ...—	...
Ellen Sydall 15	...	John Wood ... ...—	...
Humphrey Halksworth17	...	Mary Buxton, Foolow	
Martha Bands 17	...	—	...
Jonathan Ragge... ...18	...	Ann Blackwell ... ...—	...
Humphrey Torre ...19	..	Alice Halksworth ...—, 1666	
Thomas Thorpe ...19	...	Thomas Allen, April 6	...
Mary Bands 20	...	Joan Blackwell... ... 6	...
Elizabeth Sydall ...22	...	Alice Thorpe 15	...
Alice Ragge 23	...	Edward Bainsley 15 or 16	...
Alice Sydall 24	...	Margret Blackwell do.	...
George Ragge 26	...	Samuel Hadfield ...18	...
Jonathan Cooper ...28	...	Margret Gregory ...21	...
Humphrey Torre ...30	...	— Allen (an infant) 28	...
Hugh Stubbs, Nov. 1	...	Emmot Sydal 29, 1666	
Alice Teyler 3	...	Robert Thorpe, May 2	...
Hannah Rowland ... 5	...	William Thorpe ... 2	...
John Stubbs 15	...	James Teyler 11	...
Ann Stubbs (his wife)19	...	Ellen Charlesworth ...24	...
Elizabeth Warrington 29	...	Isaac Thornley, June 2	...
Randoll Daniel 30	...	Anna Thornley... ...12	...
Mary Rowland, Dec. 1	...	Jonathan Thornley ...12	...
Richard Coyle 2	...	Anthony Skidmore ...12	...
John Rowbotham ... 9	...	Elizabeth Thornley ...15	..
— Rowe (an infant) 14	...	James Mower 15	...
Mary Rowe 15	...	Elizabeth Buxton ...15	...
William Rowe 19	...	Mary Heald 16	...
Thomas Willson ...22	...	Francis Thornley ...17	...
William Rowbotham...24	...	Mary Skidmore ...17	...
Anthony Blackwell ...24	...	Sarah Lowe 17	...
Robert Rowbotham, Jan. 1, 1665-6		Mary Mellow 18	...
Samuel Rowbotham... 1	...	Anna Townsend ...19	...
Abell Rowland 15	..	Abel Archdale 20	...
John Thornley 28	...	Edward Thornley ...22	...
Isaac Willson 28	...	Ann Skidmore 24	..
Peter Mortin, Bretton Feb. 4	...	Jane Townsend... ...25	...
Thomas Rowland ...14	...	Emmot Heald 26	...
John Willson 15	...	John Swanna 29	...
Deborah Willson ...17	...	Elizabeth Heald, July 2	...
Alice Willson 18	...	William Lowe ... 2	...
Adam Halksworth .. 18	...	Eleanor Lowe (his wife) 3	...
Anthony Blackwell ...21	...	Deborah Ealott... ... 3	...
Elizabeth Abell... ...27	...	George Darby 4	...
		Anna Coyle 5	...

BURIED.	A.D.
Briget Talbot, Riley, July	... 5, 1666
Mary Talbot, Riley	... 5 ...
John Dannyell ...	... 5 ...
Elizabeth Swanna	... 6 ...
Mary Thornley. .	... 6 ..
John Townsend	... 7 ...
Ann Talbot (Riley)	... 7 ...
Francis Ragge ...	... 8 ...
Elizabeth Thorpe	... 8 ...
Elizabeth Lowe	... 9 ...
Edytha Torre ...	... 9 ...
Anne Lowe ...	...13 ...
Margret Teyler...	...14 ...
Alice Thornley...	...16 ...
Jane Naylor . .	...16 ...
Edytha Barkinge	...17 ...
Elizabeth Thornley	...17 ...
Jane Talbot ...	...17 ...
Robert Whytely	...18 ..
Catherine Talbot	...18 ...
Thomas Heald ...	...18 ...
Robert Torre ...	..18 ...
George Short ...	...18 ...
Thomas Ashe ...	...18 ...
William Thornley	...19 ...
Francis Wood ...	.. 22 ...
Thomas Thorpe	...22 ...
Robert Thorpe ...	...22 ..
Robert Talbot ...	. 24 ...
Joan Nealor ...	.. 25 ...
Thomas Healley	...25 ...
Richard Talbot..	...25 ...
John Nealor ...	...26 ...
Joan Talbot ..	...26 ...
Ruth Talbot ...	. 26 ...
Anna Chapman...	...26 ...
Lydia Chapman...	...28 ...
Margret Allen ...	...29 ...
John Torre ...	...29 ...
Samuel Ealott, ..	...29 ...
Rowland Mower	...29 ...
Thomas Barkinge	..30 ...
Nicholas Whitby	...30 ...
Jonathan Talbot	...30 ...
Mary Whitby . .	...30 ...
Rowland Mower	...30 ...

BURIED.	A.D.
Sarah Ealott ...	...31, 1666
Joseph Allen ...	...31 ...
Ann Martin, Bretton	31 ...
Robert Kempe, Shepherd's Flat ...	..31 ...
George Ashe, ...Aug.	1 ...
Mary Nealor ...	... 1 ...
John Hadfield ...	... 2 ...
Robert Buxton ...	... 2 ...
Ann Naylor ...	... 2 ...
Jonathan Naylor	... 2 ...
Elizabeth Glover ...	2 ...
Alexander Hadfield ..	3 ...
Jane Nealor ...	... 3 ...
Godfrey Torre ...	.. 3 ...
John Hancock, jun. ...	3 ...
Elizabeth Hancock ..	3 ...
Margaret Buxton ...	3 ...
Robert Barkinge ...	3 ...
Margaret Percival ...	4 ...
Ann Swinnerton ...	4 ...
Rebecca Mortin, Shepherd's Flat ...	... 4 ...
Robert French ...	... 6 ...
Richard Thorpe...	... 6 ...
Thomas Frith ...	... 6 ...
John Yealot ...	... 7 ...
Oner Hancock ...	... 7 ...
John Hancock ...	... 7 ...
William Hancock ...	7 ...
Abram Swinnerton ..	8 ...
Alice Hancock ...	... 9 ...
Ann Hancock ...	...10 ...
Frances Frith ...	...10 ...
Elizabeth Kempe	...11 ...
William Halksworth	12 ...
Thomas Kempe...	...12 ...
Francis Bocking	...13 ..
Richard Bocking	...13 ...
Mary Bocking ...	...13 ...
John Tricket ...	...13 ...
Ann Tricket (his wife)	13 ...
Mary Whitbey ..	...13 ...
Sarah Blackwall, Bretton	...13 ...
Brigett Naylor ..	...13 ...
Robert Hadfield	...14 ...

BURIED.		A.D.	BURIED.		A.D.
Margaret Swinnerton	14,	1666	William Percival, Sept.	1,	1666
Alice Coyle	14	...	Robert Trickett...	... 2	...
Thurston Whitbey	15	...	Henry Frith	... 3	...
Alice Bocking ...	...15	...	John Willson ...	... 4	...
Briget Talbot ...	...15	...	Mary Darby ...	... 4	...
Michael Kempe...	...15	...	William Abell ...	... 7	...
Ann Wilson ...	. .15	...	George Frith ...	... 7	...
Thomas Bilston..	...16	...	Godfrey Ashe ...	... 8	...
Thomas Frith ...	...17	...	William Halksworth...	9	...
Joan French ..	...17	..	Robert Wood ...	.. 9	...
Mary Yealot ...	...17	...	Humphrey Merril	... 9	...
Sarah Mortin, Shep-			Sarah Willson ...	...10	...
herd's Flat ...	...18	...	Thomas Mozley...	...16	...
Elizabeth Frith...	...18	...	Joan Wood...	...16	.
Ann Yealot ...	...18	...	Mary Percival ...	.. 18	...
Thomas Ragge ...	..18	...	Francis Mortin ...	...20	...
Ann Halksworth	...19	...	George Butterworth...21		..
Joan Ashmore ...	...19	...	Ann Townsend, Bret-		
Elizabeth Frith...	...20	...	ton	...22	...
Margaret Mortin	...20	...	Ann Glover ...	...23	...
Ann Rowland ...	...20	...	Ann Hall	...23	...
Joan Buxton ...	...20	...	Francis Halksworth	...23	..
Frances Frith ...	...21	...	– Townsend, an infant	29	...
Ruth Mortin ...	...21	...	Susanna Mortin...	...29	...
—— Frith, an infant	22	...	James Parsley ...Oct.	1	...
Lydia Kempe ...	...22	...	Grace Mortin ...	... 2	...
Peter Hall, Bretton	...23	...	Peter Ashe... ...	... 4	...
—— Mortin, an infant	24	...	Abram Mortin ...	.. 5	...
Catherine Mompesson.25		...	Thomas Torre ...	...—	—
Samuel Chapman	...25	...	Benjamin Mortin	...—	...
Ann Frith	...25	...	Elizabeth Mortin	...—	...
Joan Howe ...	.. 27	...	Alice Teyler ...	.. —	...
Thomas Ashmore	...27	...	Ann Parsley ...	...—	...
Thomas Wood ...	...28	...	Agnes Sheldon ...	...—	...
William Howe ..	..30	...	Mary Mortin ...	...—	...
Mary Abell... ...	...30	...	Samuel Hall ...	...—	..
Catherine Talbot	...30	...	Peter Hall	..—	...
Francis Wilson ...	...30	...	Joseph Mortin ...	...—	...
Elizabeth Frith.. Sept.	1	...			

The number of these hallowed names is 267;
but, as Mompesson states the precise number of
the all-glorious self-martyrs to be 259, it is thought
that eight out of the 267 died during the plague,
but not of the plague. Tradition mentions this

to be the case in two or three instances. The
Register gives no date from the fifth to the fifteenth
of October, therefore it cannot be ascertained
which of the two or three last mentioned deaths
occurred on the eleventh of October : the date of
the death of the plague's last victim. There appears to have been from the fifteenth to the last of
. October, six deaths out of the small remnant left ;
but the authority of Mompesson, for the cessation
of the pestilence on the eleventh of October, must
be conclusive and satisfactory. A very many of
the victims of the same name, are distinguished
from each other in the Register by stating their
degrees of relationship ;—this I have omitted, as
before mentioned, to avoid tedious repetition and
useless verbosity.

THE CHURCH.—This very plain fabric stands,
as I have before noticed, nearly in the centre of
the village : the churchyard wall on the south side,
running parallel with, and close by, the principal
street. It is a very simple edifice ; quite in keeping with the scenery around. That there was a
former church—perhaps as far back as Saxon
times—is highly probable : indeed, there are a few
relics about the present structure, strongly indicative of great antiquity. Almost every part of
the building is comparatively modern ; the north
part is of the reign of Henry the Second ; the
south, or front part, of Elizabeth ; the chancel was
erected about the year A.D. 1600 ; and the tower
was rebuilded about the same time. There is only
one good window in the whole structure—it is at
the east end of the north aisle, evidently of the
fourteenth century. A few specimens of painted
glass adorn this antique window.

It was a very small church previously to the ad-

dition of the chancel, which was erected by the
Rev. Robert Talbot, Rector of Eyam, at the time
afore-mentioned.   The old tower, which was but
small, was taken down, and the present one builded
by a Madam Stafford, a maiden lady, one of the
co-heiresses of Humphrey Stafford, Eyam.   The
grotesque figures projecting from the top part of
the tower, belonged to the old tower; and from
their defaced and dilapidated appearance, as com-
pared with those on the Saxon churches of Hope
and Tankersley, they must certainly have been
ornaments of a church long anterior to the Norman
Conquest.   The tower is square, nearly sixty feet
high, surmounted with small embattlements and
four ornamented pinnacles, about five feet in
length.   Four rich and deep toned bells occupy
the top part of the tower, where ten bells might be
hung conveniently.   The bells, which are said to
have been given by Madam Stafford, are rich in
material—containing much silver.   They have the
following inscriptions :—

1st. JESVS   BEE   OVR   SPEED.   1619. c o.
2nd. GOD   SAVE   HJS   CHVRCH.   1618. c o.
3rd. JESVS   BE   OVR   SPEDE,   1618. c o.
4th. JESWS   BE   OVR   SPEDE,   1628.

There are five bell frames, but never five bells,
although there is a notion prevails that one was
stolen and taken to Longstone, or elsewhere.—
Nearly in the middle of the west side of the tower
there is a stone something less than the adjoining
stones, with the following letters, and something
like figures inscribed thereon :—

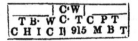

This stone, amongst the *Solons* of the village, has been the source of numberless conjectures. The letters are evidently modern in character—not more than two centuries and a half old; the date of the erection of the tower. They are most probably the initials of the then Churchwardens; this is almost certain from the C. W. at the head of the other letters. What the figures mean is totally inexplicable; for it cannot be supposed that they mean A.D. 915. Some think they are not figures at all. As I have not given the inscription in the precise character of the letters, it would, therefore be recommendable to all who are interested in mystical inscriptions, to see it before they conclude concerning it from what is here advanced.*

Notwithstanding the architectural defects of the church, it has, however, one classical ornament that would add to the splendour of some of our magnificent cathedrals. It is the sun-dial, placed immediately over the principal doorway into the church. This complex piece of mathematical ingenuity, which is one of the finest of the kind in the kingdom, was delineated by Mr. Duffin, Clerk to — Simson, Esq., formerly a worthy magistrate of Stoke Hall, near Eyam. The workmanship and engraving are by the late Mr. William Shore, of Eyam, an ingenious stone-mason. The following is a brief description of its admirable contents, by an able hand at gnomonics :—" It is a vertical plane declining westward, and from certain mathe-

---

* It is the opinion of a many that this stone is of great antiquity. It evidently was either intended for a different situation, or it belonged to the old tower—if the latter, it is very old, notwithstanding the letters being so very perfect. In the *British Magazine* for 1832, vol. 2nd, there is a *fac simile* of the inscription.

matical principles connected with conic sections, the parallels of the sun's declination for every month in the year—a scale of the sun's meridian altitude—an azimuthal scale—the points of the compass, and a number of meridians are well delineated on the plane from the stereographic projection of the sphere.

" The plane being large the horary scale is well divided; the upper, or fiducial edge of the style is of brass, and an indentation therein representing the centre of the projection, casts the light or shade of its point on the hyperbolic curves and other furniture of the dial." How lamentable that this noble work of genius should stand in its present neglected state! Much of the exterior of the south side of this edifice is covered with ivy, which, if not immediately checked, will soon envelope the whole structure.

The interior consists of nave, chancel, and north and south aisles. The chancel is open to the body of the church only by an arch, which intercepts to some degree the intended and necessary connection. The modern erection of a south side gallery, and one of rather older date, at the western extremity, have lamentably destroyed the original. architectural beauty of the church. Seven pointed arches, three on the north side, three on the south side, and one on the west end, supported by plain, octagonal, and clustered pillars, once adorned the interior of this edifice. Two only now visibly remain. How deplorable that the whims and fancies of some persons should be allowed to destroy the ornaments and designs of our pious and venerable forefathers.

An ancient stone font, lined with lead, occupies its wonted place; and strongly reminds us of the simplicity of past times. There are also a few relics of Catholic times. At the north-east extremity of the church, there are the remains of the Confessional. An aperture in the wall is still seen, through which, it is said, were whispered the confession of sins. And at the same place, a small stone projects from the wall, with a hollow or cavity for the holy-water. Some have imagined that there were another Confessional, or place of priestly officiation, on the opposite side of the church; but of this there is scarcely any trace; and, indeed, were it so, it would intimate that the church had at one time two priests, which is hardly probable. Of the monuments and other things of interest in the interior, there are but few of importance. On the top of the roof of the chancel, there is carved, in wood, a talbot, or dog, which is a supporter of the arms of the Earls of Shrewsbury, who were Lords of the Manor of Eyam, and patrons of the living. The inscription, J. B., 1595, F. B., may be seen on the front of the manorial seat: the letters are the initials of John Bradshaw and Francis Bradshaw. This family succeeded to the family mansion and part of the estate of the Staffords, who are supposed to be interred under the manorial pew. There is no monument, however, of this once influential family, which may be accounted for, through the church having been, in this and other parts, frequently altered; when, as no branch of the family dwelled at Eyam any length of time, after the death of the coheiresses of the last male of the Staffords, anything commemorative of their memories would probably be destroyed. The old manorial pew was remodelled and repaired by the Bradshaws.

In the chancel there is a mural monument, to

L

the memory of John Wright, gentleman, who was
buried January 2d, 1694; and Elizabeth, his wife,
buried August 22d, 1700.   The inscription is
surmounted by the family arms.   Two others, to
the ancestors and other relatives of M. M. Middleton, Esq. of Leam Hall.   One to Ralph Rigby,
curate of Eyam twenty-two years, buried April
22, 1740.*   A brass plate, to the memory of A.
Hamilton, Rector of Eyam, who was buried,
October 21, 1717.   The inscription is in Latin.
Another brass plate commemorates the memory of
Bernard, son of Bernard Wells, who died March
16th, 1648.   An alabaster monument of great
beauty perpetuates the memory of Mary, daughter
of Smithson Green, Esq., Brosterfield, who died in
May, 1777.   In the vestry there is a brass plate to
the memories of Charles Hargrave, Rector of Eyam,
who died Nov. 18, 1822; and to his son William,
who died Nov. 1st, 1816.   A stone in an obscure
corner records the death of Joseph Hunt, Rector
of Eyam, who was buried December 16, 1709;
and Ann, his wife, buried December 18th, 1703.
In the manorial pew there is a brass plate, to the
memory of John Galliard, who died April 29, 1745.
On the opposite side of the pillar there is another,
adorned with a death's head and cross bones, to
the memory of John Willson, who died December
21, 1716.   On the reading desk there is a plate to
the memory of the Rev. Edmund Fletcher, who
died Oct. 7th, 1745.   These, with a few other
slabs on the floor, are all of any moment in the

* The night of the funeral of this Rev. Divine was attended
with the following singular occurrence:—Three clergymen, from
Yorkshire, returning from the funeral, was lost on the East
Moor in a snow, which fell after the setting of the sun. A
shepherd found one on the following morning, and with difficulty
animation was restored; the other two were dead when found.

church. There is one unassuming stone, however, laid flat in the chancel, simply inscribed with T. B., the initials of Thomas Birds, Esq., Eyam, of antiquarian notoriety: he died May 25th, 1828. The national arms ; a full length figure of Aaron and Moses, painted in oil in the reign of Queen Anne ; a table of benefactions, the Lord's [prayer and belief, are, with the exception of an organ, erected a few years ago, all the other principal ornaments of the interior of this holy edifice. In justice it must be observed, that notwithstanding the humble exterior and interior of the church, it is exceeded by no place of worship in the kingdom in order, cleanliness, and in the due observance of its services, as respects the present Reverend Pastors.

THE CHURCHYARD. If it be possible to be in love with death, it certainly must be while gazing on the daisy-clad graves of this lovely, green church-yard. Ah! 'tis here,

> —— the dead returns to dust,
> In Nature's own befitting way ;
> Earth o'er them throws a mantling robe,
> Of flowers both sweet and gay.

The towering, leafy, linden trees, which encompass this church-yard, have often and invariably called forth the admiration of strangers. They were planted at the suggestion or wish of one of the ancestors of John Wright, Esq., Eyam,—his grandfather, I believe. They have, however, been deemed a nuisance, and one half have been felled about two years ago, to the great regret of the parishioners in general. Notwithstanding this affectionate regard, it must be admitted that the lopping down of every other has greatly improved the church as a striking feature in the landscape, besides adding to the airiness and lightsomeness of the church-yard.

Amongst the prominent and generally interesting objects of this place of village sepulchre is, the tomb of Mrs. Mompesson,

" Where tears have rained, nor yet shall cease to flow."
WILLIAM AND MARY HOWITT.

Ah ! what numbers have I seen bending over this hallowed tomb, chained as it were to the spot, by emotions the most intense and overwhelming. O! what a glorious and convincing evidence is this of the immortal sympathy which exists in the souls of beings created in the image of God, and destined to live eternally after death.

The inscription on the top of the tomb is in Latin—the following is a translation :—" Catherine, wife of William Mompesson, Rector of this church, daughter of Ralph Carr, Esq., late of Cocken, in the county of Durham. She was buried on the 25th day of August, 1666 ! Take heed for ye know not the hour." On one end of the tomb is an hour glass, between two expanded wings, intended to represent the rapid flight of time; underneath, on an oblong tablet, Cave* is inscribed; and nearer the base appears the words *Nescites Horam*. On the other end of the tomb is a death's head, resting on a plain projecting tablet, below which are the words *Mihi lucrum*, nearly obliterated. At the corners of the tomb are four rude stone pillars; and at the east end a yew tree has been planted by the present Rector, the Rev. E. B. Bagshaw.

Opposite the chancel door, and very near the tomb of Mrs. Mompesson, is the old stone cross,

which has found a place in the sketch books of
numberless visitors and admirers. It is about eight
feet high, although about a foot of the shaft is
broken and lost. A variety of figures and designs
are embossed thereon, with a many singular symbolical devices. What are said to be *Runic* and
Scandinavian knots, liberally adorn its sides. No
cross, perhaps, in England, is more richly embel-
lished. It would be difficult, amongst so many
conflicting opinions on the subject, to say anything
correct respecting the origin of crosses. Some
give them a Danish and some a Saxon origin: they
are, most probably, no older than the time of the
Crusades. Rhodes, in the Peak Scenery, states
that the top part of this cross lay in the church-
yard, covered with docks and thistles, when
Howard, the philanthropist, was at Eyam; and
that he caused it to be placed on the dilapidated
shaft. This is a mistake. The top part may
have been some time from its proper place, but it
was before Howard's time. This venerable relic
of antiquity was, a few years since, raised up and
placed upon a kind of pedestal for its better preservation and appearance.

This church-yard has often and justly been
styled poetic ground; "scarcely a stone but has
its distich commemorative of the virtues of the
deceased, and the sorrows of surviving relatives."
Near the tomb of Mrs. Mompesson, and close
by the chancel door, there is an humble upright stone, with the following quaint inscription:—

Here lieth the body of Ann Sellars,
Buried by this stone—who
Died on Jan. 15th day, 1731.
Likewise here lise dear Isaac
Sellars, my husband and my right,
Who was buried on that same day come

Seven years, 1738. In seven years
Time there come a change—
Observe and here you'll see,
On that same day come
Seven years my husband's
Laid by me.

WRITTEN BY ISAAC SELLARS.

Numberless are the stones in this burial place that contain the offerings of the muse of the Rev. R. Cunningham, curate of Eyam church from 1772 to 1790. Close adjoining the south side of the steeple, or tower, is the burial place of the Sheldons, Eyam, the maternal ancestors of Thomas Fentem, Esq., surgeon, of Eyam Terrace. Their tombs, under which is the vault, are paled off with metal palisading—very neatly. Affixed to the tower, just over the tombs, is a stone, containing the following lines, partly from Shakspere's Cymbeline :—

" Elizth. Laugher, Ob. Feb. 4th, 1741, Æt. 24.
  Fear no more the heat o' th' sun,
  Nor the furious winter's rages,
  Thou thy worldly task hast done,
  Home art gone and ta'en thy wages.
  I weep thee now, but I too must,
  Here end with thee and turn to dust ;
  In Christ may endless union prove,
  The consummation of our love.
    Erected by Tho. Sheldon. (Her Lover.")

The following epitaph, written by him whom it commemorates, cannot but be recognized as a mutilated quotation from a fine passage in Homer's Iliad. The sense is reversed and in every respect spoiled :—

" William Talbot, died April 16, 1817, aged 79 years.
  Cold death o'ertook him in his *aged years,*
  And left *no parents* unavailing tears ;
  Relations now enjoy his worldly store—
  The *race* forgotten and the name no more."

Spencer T. Hall, in his incomparable " Ram-

bles in the Country," thus beautifully alludes to
this church-yard:—" A cemetery more indicative
of local history and character than this, it would
be difficult to find perhaps in the whole of England; and I never read a more interesting chapter
of village biography than here."

RECTORS. The Register, in which there is
nearly all that can be found respecting the names
and dates of the succession of the Rectors, is
astonishingly deficient in information on this head.
By reference to other sources, and what the Register affords, I am still only able to give the following imperfect account, as respects the time
when they succeeded each other. Nor have I
been more successful in attempting to get the
names of those who preceded the first on the following list :—

	Died.	Died or Resigned.	Suspended.	Resigned.
Rev. Robert Talbot	1630			
Rev. Sherland Adams			1644	
Rev. Thomas Stanley...				1662
Rev. Sherland Adams (again)	1664			
Rev. William Mompesson				1669
Rev. Henry Adams or Oldham...		1675		
Rev. —— Ferns		1679		
Rev. —— Carver*				
Rev. Joseph Hunt	1709			
Rev. —— Hawkins				1711
Rev. Alexander Hamilton...	1717			
Rev. Dr. Edmund Finsh	1737			
Rev. —— Bruce	1739			
Rev. Thomas Seward...	1790			
Rev. Charles Hargrave	1822			
Hon. Rev. Robert Eden				1826
Rev. Edward B. Bagshaw, Present Rector				
Rev. J. Casson, Curate				

* This Rector was of the family of Carvers, of Whiston,
Yorkshire, of whom M. M. Middleton, Esq., Leam Hall, is a
descendant.

Of these Rectors, only a few have been particularly distinguished. The Rev. Robert Talbot, whose name is the first in the oldest Register, was of the family of the Talbots, Earls of Shrewsbury. The Talbots of Eyam, of whom the last of the name died in 1817, were descended from this Rector, and were consequently of the same aristocratical blood.*

The Rev. Sherland Adams, was Rector of Eyam, and also of Treeton, in Yorkshire. His numerous and vexatious suits at law with the parishioners of Eyam, rendered him extremely hated; and his conduct at Treeton, where he chiefly resided, was no less disreputable. When the war broke out between King Charles and the Parliament, his intolerance and party spirit became ungovernable; and his furious loyalty assumed such an aspect, that he was regarded with disgust. The measures he took in favour of the royal cause, excited the notice of the partizans of the Parliament, and he was seized, deprived of his livings, and cast into prison. The charges preferred against him are embodied in a pamphlet, written by one Nicholas Ardron, of Treeton, the only copy of which, now known, is in the British Museum. One of the accusations is as follows:—
" Further, it is charged against him, that he is a man much given to much trouble and suits at law, as is well known at Eyam, in Derbyshire, where he was Rector, where they tasted of this his turbulent spirit; that he gave tythe of lead ore to the King against the Parliament, delivered a man and musket against them, and sent a fat ox to the

* I have not any direct proof of what is here advanced, but it is almost certain. And I noticed in looking over the genealogy of the Earls of Shrewsbury, that the adopted names of the minor members were Richard, Robert, and William—the Talbots of Eyam were the same.

Earl of Newcastle, as a free gift to maintain the
war against the Parliament." He was amongst
the number of gentlemen who compounded for
their estates. For a small estate at Woodlathes,
near Conisbro', he paid £198, where he resided
until the restoration, when he was restored to his
livings again. That this Rev. Divine, was a dis-
grace to his order, may be satisfactorily seen, from
the following extra evidence :—When the Rev. —
Fowler, Sheffield, gave up his living for non-conformity, Sherland said that, " Fowler was a fool,
for before he would have lost his on that account,
he would have sworn a black crow was white."*
How glaring and striking the contrast between
this conforming hypocrite, and the virtuous, non-
conformist, Stanley. Adams died April 11th,
1664, and was buried in the chancel of the Church
at Treeton, where a Latin epitaph commemorates
his loyalty, *virtues*, and sufferings.

The Rev. Thomas Stanley, whose memory is
still cherished in Eyam and its vicinity, with a degree of adoration which rarely falls to the lot of
any public man, was translated to the living of
Eyam, in the year 1644, immediately after the
arrest of Sherland Adams, the *bona fide* Rector.
He continued in his office, beloved and respected,
until Bartholomew-day, 1662. It was in the
capacity of Curate, however, that he officiated
from 1660 to 1662. Sherland Adams, having obtained possession of his livings at the restoration,
in 1660. After enduring, for a few years, the
sneers and bickering of a few bitter enemies,
Stanley laid his head on the pillow of death, encircled with an halo of consolation, arising from
an uncorrupted heart and an unviolated conscience.

* Vide Hunter's History of Hallamshire.

He was buried at Eyam, where he died, August, 1670. During the time of this holy man's ministry at Eyam, he performed the part of lawyer in the making of wills, and in numerous other matters. In his hand writing there are still extant numerous testamentary documents, and his signature is attached to many important deeds of conveyance, all tending to prove his high esteem—his honour and unimpeachable probity. He was supported by the voluntary contributions of two-thirds of the parishioners. Let it be understood, however, that the high character here given of Stanley, is from the consideration of his sterling virtues, and not from his non-conformity, of the nature of which, I have but a faint knowledge. Of his successor, Mompesson, enough can never be said in his praise.

The Rev. Joseph Hunt has rendered his name somewhat particular, by an ill-judged, and disgraceful act, during his ministry at Eyam. The circumstance, although but little known now, is, however, well authenticated, and is as follows:— A party of miners had assembled at the Miners' Arms Inn, Eyam, the house now occupied by Mr. John Slinn; it was kept by a Matthew Ferns, and an infant child of his being suddenly taken ill, the rector, Hunt, was sent for to baptise it immediately. Having performed the ceremony he was invited to sit and regale himself with the boozing bacchanalians—the miners. This, it appears, he did until he was inebriated. The landlord had a very handsome daughter about eighteen, and Hunt, inspired by John Barleycorn, began to speak out in luscious commendation of her charms. From one thing to another, it was at last agreed that Hunt should marry her; and the miners, not

willing to trust him to fulfil his engagement another
time, insisted that the ceremony should take place
there and then. To this, after taking another
glass, he unfortunately consented. The common
prayer book was brought out, and one of the miners
put on a solemn aspect, and read the whole ceremony: Hunt and the happy damsel performing
their respective parts. After the affair had spread
round the neighbourhood, it at last reached the
ears of the Bishop of the Diocese, who threatened
to suspend him if he did not fulfil in earnest what
he had done in jest. He was therefore obliged to
marry Miss Ferns, legally. This, however, was
not the last of his misfortunes, arising from the
affair: he was under promise of marriage to a
young lady, near Derby, who immediately commenced an action against him for breach of promise. Some years were passed in litigation, which
drained his purse and estranged his friends; and
eventually, he had to take shelter in the vestry
(which, I think, was built for that purpose), where
he resided the remainder of his life, to keep the
law-hounds at bay. He died in this humble ap-
pendage to the church, where his bones and those
of his wife lie buried. He is represented to have
been very social—the young men of the village
visited him in his solitary abode, where they sat
round the fire, telling alternate tales to *while* away
the dreary winter nights. This improvident marriage was attended with its natural consequence—
poverty: he had a large family; and one of his
descendants is now one of the most celebrated
cricket-players in England; and another, a female
belonging to Eyam, is now an inmate of the Bakewell Union Workhouse.

The Rev. — Hawkins succeeded Hunt; but

he only tarried in Eyam two years. He exchanged his living with the Rev. Alexander Hamilton, just before the rich vein of lead ore, commonly called the edge-side vein, came into Eyam liberty. The great profit accruing to the Rector from this circumstance, induced Hawkins to regret his exchange; and he, eventually, but unsuccessfully, used every possible means to annul his contract.

Dr. Edmund Finch, brother of Finch, the Earl of Nottingham, uncle and guardian to the daughters and coheiresses of William Saville, Marquis of Halifax, succeeded Hamilton, as Rector of Eyam. He left the great living of Wigan for the then very rich living of Eyam. During the twenty years he was Rector, he resided but little at Eyam. He gave the very handsome service of communion plate; and was otherwise a benefactor.*

The Rev. — Bruce succeeded Finch. The living was presented to him while he was abroad. He died of brain fever, while returning in haste to take possession of his living.

The Rev. Thomas Seward was Rector from the death of Bruce in 1739 to 1790. He became, in 1772, Canon of Lichfield; but still held the living of Eyam. The Rev. Peter Cunningham, poet, was his curate. During his residence in Lichfield, he made an annual visit to Eyam; and was frequently drawn in his carriage into Eyam by the rejoicing villagers, whom he invariably recompensed by the distribution of a well fed carcase of beef.

The Rev. Charles Hargrave succeeded Seward. Troubles connected with his mode of obtaining the

* The great-great-grandfather of the author of this work, came with Finch, from Wigan, as a servant:—he was a young man; he married, had a family, and died in Eyam. Hence the origin of the author's family in Eyam; and hence their attachment to the Established Church.

living harrassed him for some years. The matter
was at length settled; and he lived thirty-two
years as pastor, respected, loved, and deservedly
esteemed.

The Hon. and Rev. Robert Eden, his successor,
has left an indelible trace of sincere respect on the
heart of every inhabitant of Eyam. He resigned
the living in 1826; and his farewell sermon on the
occasion drew from his sobbing audience a shower
of tears. Since his departure he has, however,
visited at intervals his former and affectionate
flock; when he has had the satisfaction to see how
highly he is still esteemed by the villagers of Eyam.
The Rev. E. B. Bagshaw succeeded him, and is
now the present Rector of Eyam.

THE LIVING, on account of the mines, varies in
its annual amount. One penny for every dish of
ore is due to the Rector; and twopence farthing
for every load of hillock-stuff. During the greater
part of the last century the living was worth from
a £1000 to £2000 a year. Little, however, is
now derived from the mines; but it is likely,
should the speculations now in progress to liberate
the mines from water, be carried into effect, that
this benefice may become as valuable again, or
even more so. It is now worth about £300 a
year: near two-thirds of which is derived from
glebe lands, and the remainder from tythes and
surplice fees.

THE REGISTER contains but few matters worth
transcribing. The following are the most particular:—" December 30th, 1663, buried Anna the
traveller, who according to her own account, was
136 years of age. Edward Torre, June 30th,
1699, killed with a plugg over against the parson's
fold. Elizabeth, the wife of John Trout, died in a

M

snow near Sir William, as she was returning from Tideswell market, Feb. 4th, 1692. John White, found dead in the Dale, Feb. 18th, 1695." These are the few most prominent events recorded in the Register. I will, however, give one more extract strikingly indicative of the simplicity of the mode in which our village forefathers characterized each other :—" Old Robert Slinn, died 26th of November, 1692." How patriarchal! How much in keeping "with the spirit and manners of the locality," is this old man's distinction from others.

THE MINES. There is, particularly on the south side of Eyam, strong evidence of much mining in past ages. Indeed, the Eyam Mineral Charter proves the antiquity of the lead mines at Eyam. This village and parish is included under the general denomination of the KING's FIELD, which is subject to the operation of a peculiar system of mineral law. One clause of the law declares, " that by the custom of the mine it is lawful for *all* the King's liege subjects to dig, delve, search, subvert, and overturn, all manner of grounds, lands, meadows, closes, pastures, mears, and marshes, for ore mines, of *whose inheritance soever they be ;* dwelling houses, orchards, and gardens, excepted." From the inconvenient effects of this sweeping clause many of the old freehold tenures of the parish of Eyam, are exempt, through the virtue of a charter granted by King John, previously to his being created Duke of Lancaster. Who holds this charter now, I am not aware, neither can any person name the particular tenures alluded to. They are, however, supposed to be those contiguous to the village : or what is denominated the old land. With the exception of a little land at Hucklow, and at Grippe,

these decreed tenures at Eyam, are the only lands
exempted from the arbitrary mineral laws, observed throughout the comprehensive district of a
great part of the Peak of Derbyshire.

Of the ore obtained from the mines in the whole
parish of Eyam, the *lot*, which is every thirteenth
dish, is claimed and taken by the Lords of the
Manor. One penny a dish belongs to the Rector;
and a small exaction called *cope*, is paid by the
purchaser of the ore to the Barmaster: these,
with a trifle paid to the Rector, and the Lords of
the Manor, for what is provincially called hillock-
stuff, are the lots and tythes paid by the mines of
Eyam.

The Lords of the Manors of Eyam and Stoney
Middleton, held an half-yearly court, alternately
at Eyam and Stoney Middleton. This court is
denominated the Great Court Barmoot, at which
the steward, — Charge, Esq., Chesterfield, pre-
sides, who with twenty-four jurymen, chosen every
half-year, determine all cases of disputes that occur, respecting the working of the mines in the
above Manors. Other matters, independent of
mines, are also adjusted at these periodical courts,
of which, the whole expences, are paid by the
Lords of the Manors. The Barmaster, M. Frost,
Esq., Baslow, has also important offices connected
with the mines: putting miners into the possession
of new discovered mines, collecting the lots due to
the Lords of the Manors, and measuring all the
ore, are only a few of the Barmaster's duties.

The great vein of ore, known as the Edge-side
vein, was discovered about a century and a half
ago; but it was not worked in the parish of Eyam,
until some time after its discovery. In the space
of fifty or sixty years, it was cut for more than

two miles in length; but dipping very fast eastward, it at last reached the water, and could no longer be successfully worked. A sough or level was brought up to it from the river Derwent, about eighty years since, but did not answer general expectation. The quantity of metal obtained from this vein, may be judged of, from the fact, that it enhanced the annual income of the Rector, from £1200 to £1800 a year, and this for a long time. Other veins in the vicinity have been very productive; but nearly all have been long shut up by the same, almost irresistable element—water. The water-groove mine, just within the parish of Eyam, is by far the richest in the neighbourhood. A steam engine of three hundred horse power has been just erected on this mine, and it is anxiously hoped that it will be able to compete with the water. Lumps of metal, from three to five hundred weight are often obtained from this very rich lead mine. By far the oldest lead works are of the *rake* kind, extending over a large tract of land south of the village. And, as I have before observed, the village, in a great measure, stands on the ruins of old mines; all tending to prove the great antiquity of the lead works at Eyam. Camden thinks that Derbyshire was alluded to by Pliny, when he says, " In Britain, lead is found near the surface of the earth in such abundance, that a law is made to limit the quantity which shall be gotten."

Of the origin of the laws and customs connected with the working of the lead mines in Eyam and its vicinity there is much room for speculation. Some think that they originated with the original inhabitants of Derbyshire; but from a passage in Suetonius, it is inferred that the mineral customs and laws of the aboriginals were superseded by others introduced by the Romans. Heineccius countenances the supposition, that private adventurers were afterwards permitted to work the mines, which would be productive of multifarious laws and regulations, and hence their anomalous character.

Bole-hills are innumerable in the vicinage of Eyam—they were the places where the ore was smelted, before the introduction of the Cupulo.

The mines in Eyam-edge are very deep, and the New-engine mine I have heard stated as being the deepest in Derbyshire. Among the number in the edge is the Hay-cliff; a mine distinguished for having contained in great abundance of that extraordinary phenomenon in the mineral world, provincially called SLICKENSIDES. It is a species of Gelena; and is well-known amongst mineralogists. This mine once had it in singular quantity and quality. The effects of this mineral are terrific: a blow with a hammer, a stroke or scratch with the miner's pick, are sufficient to blast asunder the massive rocks to which it is found attached. One writer says, " The stroke is immediately succeeded by a crackling noise, accompanied with a noise not unlike the mingled hum of a swarm of bees: shortly afterwards an explosion follows, so loud and appalling, that even the miners, though a hardy race of men, and little accustomed to fear, turn pale and tremble at the shock." Of the nature of this mineral, and its terrible power, there have been a many, but quite unsatisfactory solutions. Whitehurst, in his work on the formation of the Earth, thus mentions its wonderful power :—" In the year 1738, an explosion took place at the Hay-cliff mine, Eyam, by the power of Slickensides.

Two hundred barrels of materials were blown out at one blast—each barrel containing 350 lbs. weight. During the explosion the earth shook as by an earthquake." A person of the name of Higginbotham once but narrowly escaped with life, by striking incautiously this substance in the above mine. Experienced miners can, however, work where it greatly abounds, without much danger. It is also known by the name of CRACKING-WHOLE.

In this mine and many others in Eyam-edge, was sensibly felt the earthquake which destroyed Lisbon, on Saturday, November 1st, 1755. The following is a narrative of the occurrence, compressed from an account written by Mr. Francis Mason, an intelligent overseer of the mines in Eyam-edge at the time mentioned:— " About eleven o'clock in the forenoon of the first of November, 1755, as Francis Mason was sitting in a small room at the distance of from forty to fifty yards from the mouth of one of the engine shafts, he felt the shock of an earthquake, so violent that it raised him up in his chair, and shook some pieces of lime and plaster from the sides and roof of his little hovel. In a field about three hundred yards from the mine he afterwards observed a chasm, or cleft, in the earth, which he supposed was made at the same time : its direction was parallel to the vein of ore the miners were then pursuing, and its continuation from one extremity to the other was nearly one hundred and fifty yards. Two miners, who were employed in the drifts about sixty fathoms deep when the earthquake took place, were so terrified at the shock, that they dared not attempt to climb the shaft, which they dreaded might run in upon them, and entomb them alive. They felt themselves surrounded with danger, and as

they were conversing with each other on the means
of safety, and looking for a place of refuge, they
were alarmed by a second shock, much more violent than the one preceding. They now ran precipitately to the interior of the mine : it was an in-
stinctive movement that no way bettered their
condition; it only changed the spot of earth where
they had previously stood; but their danger and
their fears were still the same. Another shock
ensued, and after an awful and almost breathless
interval of four or five minutes, a fourth and afterwards a fifth succeeded. Every repercussion was
followed by a loud rumbling noise, which continued for about a minute; then gradually de-
creasing in force, like the thunder retiring into
distance, it subsided into an appalling stillness
more full of terror than the sounds which had
passed away, leaving the mind unoccupied by other
impressions, to contemplate the mysterious nature
of its danger. The whole space of time included
between the first and the last shock was nearly
twenty minutes. When the men had recovered a
little from their trepidation, they began to examine
the passages, and to endeavour to extricate themselves from their confinement. As they passed
along the drifts, they observed that pieces of mine-
rals were scattered along the floor, which had been
shaken from the sides and the roof, but all the
shafts remained entire and uninjured." A few
years before this earthquake, another was very
sensibly felt at Eyam. It happened on the wakes
Sunday, and the inhabitants were in the church,
when the shock came on. Several had their
prayer-books knocked from their hands by the
shock; and the pewter plates tingled on the
shelves of the houses in and around Eyam.

In bringing this brief account of the mines to a conclusion, it may not be improper to notice, that a many miners have fallen a sacrifice in pursuing their perilous and hazardous occupation.   The following are those, now remembered, with the names of the mines where they were killed :—

Edward Torre, killed near the Parson's Fold, A.D. 1669.
Three men, Stoke Sough, 80 years since,
William Fox, Shaw Engine, 90 do.
Edward, Dooley, Twelve Meers.
Robert Unwin,   do.
Michael Walker,   do.
Nineteen men, Middleton Engine, (different times.)
—— Bramwell, Twelve Meers.
—— Simson,   do.
—— Bennet, New Engine.
—— Fearest, Stoke Sough.
Samuel Howard, Water Grove.
William Hancock,   do.
A man, Broadlow.
A lad,   do.
George Benson, Pasture Grove.
—— Stailey, Twelve Meers.
—— Middleton, Mowerwood Engine.
Robert Middleton, Slater's Engine.
Francis Mower, Haycliff.

MINSTRELS. — JOHN NIGHTBRODER, although not known as a minstrel, was, however, a highly celebrated literary character, and a liberal benefactor.   He was born at Eyam, and founded the house of Carmellites, or White Friars, at Doncaster, in the year, A.D. 1350.*

MISS ANNA SEWARD, the well known poetess, was born at Eyam, in the year A.D. 1747.   In the literary world she is still distinguished, not only for her poetical powers; but for her biographical and epistolary talents.   Her father, the Rev. Thomas Seward, Rector of Eyam, prebendary of Salisbury, and canon residentiary of Lichfield, was a man of

* Vide Hunter's Deanery of Doncaster.

considerable learning and taste. In 1750, he published an edition of the plays of Beaumont and Fletcher; he was also the author of an ingenious tract on the conformity of Paganism and Popery; and in the second volume of Dodsley's Collection he published a few little, elegant poems. Is it not natural to suppose, then, that his far famed daughter first tasted of the divine fountain of poesy from the cup of his own presenting? At the age of three, before she could read, he had taught her to lisp the Allegro and Penseroso of Milton; and in her ninth year she could repeat from memory, with varied and correct accent, the three first books of Paradise Lost. In her seventh year, she left Eyam; and a few years after she removed with her father from Lichfield to Bishop's-place, where she resided until her death. She had several sisters and one brother, but all died in their infancy, excepting the second daughter, who lived till the age of nineteen. Miss Seward's intellectual precosity was zealously cherished by her admiring father; but as she advanced into womanhood, he withdrew that animating welcome which he had given to the first efforts of her muse. For awhile her productions were confined to the perusal of her intimate friends; but on her becoming acquainted with Lady Miller, of Bath Easton, she was induced to write for the poetic institution of that villa, and to become a candidate for its myrtle wreath: this she repeatedly obtained: and thus, Miss Seward, first entered into the temple of undying fame.

It is unnecessary to enumerate her works—they are well and deservedly known. The " Elegy to Major Andre," the " Death of Captain Cook," the poetical novel " Louisa," the " Epic Ode on the return of General Elliott from Gibraltar," are

amongst the best of her productions. In private
life she was much esteemed; and as an author,
totally free from that contemptible envy which too
frequently detracts from contemporary merit. Of
her enduring attachment to Eyam, the place of her
birth, she often and warmly dilated; and an annual visit to her birth-place, was the invariable
testimony of her enthusiastic affection. On her
journey through Derbyshire, to a musical festival
at Sheffield, in the summer of 1788, she visited
Eyam, and wrote the following ode, which has
never before appeared in print. The original
manuscript was in the hands of T. Birds, Esq.,
Eyam, who, before his death, kindly permitted a
friend to make a transcript from which this copy
has been taken:—

ELGIAC ODE.

" A little while I leave with anxious heart,
Source of my filial cares, thee FULL OF DAYS;
Lur'd by a promise from harmonic art
To breathe her Handel's rich, immortal lays.
Pensive I trace the Derwent's amber wave,
Winding through sylvan banks; and view it lave
The soft luxuriant valleys, high o'er-peer'd
By hills and rocks in solemn grandeur reer'd.

" Not two short miles from thou, can I refrain
Thy haunts my native EYAM, long unseen.
Thou and thy loved inhabitants again
Shall meet my transient gaze. Thy rocky screen—
Thy airy cliffs I mount and seek thy shade—
Thy roofs that brow the steep romantic glade—
But while on me the eye of Friendship glow,
Swell my pain'd sighs, my tears spontaneous flow.

" In scenes paternal not beheld through years,
Nor seen till now but by my Father's side;
Well might the tender tributary tears,
From the keen pang of duteous fondness glide;
Its Pastor to this human flock no more,
Shall the long flight of future days restore;
Distant he droops—and that once gladdening eye,
Now languid gleams e'en when his friends are nigh.

" Through this known* walk where weedy gravel lies,
Rough and unsightly ;—by the long course grass
Of the once smooth and verdant green with sighs
To the deserted rectory I pass.
The naked gloomy chambers where I found
Childhood's first bliss, my slow steps wander round ;
How chang'd since once the lightsome walls beneath,
The social joys did their warm comforts breathe.

" Yet ere I go—who may return no more,
That sacred dome mid yonder shadowy trees,
Let me revisit :—ancient, massy door ;
Thou greatest hoarse :—my vital spirits freeze
Passing the vacant pulpit, to the space
Where humble rails the decent altar grace,
And where my infant sisters' ashes sleep,†
Whose loss I left the childish sports to weep.

" Now the low beams ; with paper garlands hung
In memory of some village youth or maid ;
Draw the soft tear from thrill'd remembrance sprung
How oft my childhood marked that tribute paid :
The gloves suspended by the garlands side,
White as its snowy flowers, with ribbons tied ;
Dear village ! long these wreaths funereal spread,
Simple memorials of the early dead.

" But O ! thou blank and silent pulpit, thou
That with a father's precept just and bland,
Didst win my ear as Reason's strengthening glow,
Shewed their full value now thou seem'st to stand
Before these eyes, suffus'd with gushing tears,
Thou dearest relic of departed years ;
Of eloquence paternal, nervous, clear,
Dim remonition thou, and bitter is my tear."*

This highly celebrated lady died at Bishop's
Place, in A.D. 1809, and in the sixty-second year
of her age. Her remains repose at Lichfield.

* The Parsonage garden.

† Two of the author's little sisters lie buried in the Chancel of
Eyam Church ; but no stone or inscription marks the place
where they sleep.

* The sense in a many of the lines is exceedingly obscure.
The ode most probably was written in haste, and never amended.

The Rev. P. CUNNINGHAM, who was officiating
curate at Eyam Church a many years during the
latter part of the Rectorship of the Rev. T.
Seward, was once greatly celebrated as a poet :
and deservedly so, although his productions were
far from voluminous.   It was chiefly, if not wholly
while he resided at Eyam, that his muse, inspired
by the romantic grandeur of the surrounding "dells
and woodlands wild," wandered forth by Derwent's
stream, and there enraptured heard,

> " The red-breast, hid in golden foliage, pour
> Slow warbled requiems o'er the dying year."
>
> CHATSWORTH.

Of the parentage of Cunningham but very little
is now known in Eyam.   That he had received a
highly classical education his poetical works very
plainly indicate : and his frequent allusions to the
classics are, in general, heightened by original
comparisons.   To his favourite river, Derwent, he
thus pays " an elegant tribute" :—

> " The muse,
> She wanders, Derwent ! where, with lingering pride,
> The amber-tressed Naiads of thy stream
> Through bending woods and vales luxuriant glide.
> Fair, when the parting sun's mild golden light
> A mellower radiance on thy bosom throws,
> But fairer when the silver beams of night,
> With trembling lustre, on thy stream repose.
> " On Latmos thus, as Grecian bards have sung,
> When Night's fair Queen forsook her starry road,
> And o'er Endymion's face enamoured hung,
> His sleeping form with silver radiance glow'd."
>
> CHATSWORTH.

This is a very beautiful comparison, and original.
The whole poem is in a great measure equally
good : strongly filled with " music, image, sentiment, and thought."   There are, however, some
slight blemishes : as in one of the stanzas here

quoted, where the " *Naiads*" are made to " *glide*"
instead of the " *river*." This production was, I
believe, the first he published.

Cunningham's next poem, " THE RUSSIAN PRO-
PHECY," was written in A.D. 1785 ; and was occasioned by a phenomenon which appeared in the
heavens, but was only observed in Russia.*

THE NAVAL TRIUMPH is one of his happiest efforts, which, with the former two, constitute nearly
the whole of his poetical effusions, composed at
Eyam.

Perhaps no village pastor was ever so beloved,
by the flock committed to his charge, as Cunningham was by the inhabitants of Eyam : his memory
is still cherished, with endearing affection, notwithstanding more than half a century has elapsed
since he so reluctantly left the place. His farewell sermon, and the effect it produced on the sobbing audience, is still remembered, and frequently
mentioned. It was a composition full of eloquence,
powerful pathos, recollected kindness, and delivered in the tenderest tones of affection. Some
few copies in manuscript are still extant; and " *are
preserved with a sort of religious veneration.*"
After having preached farewell sermons in some of
the churches of the approximate villages, where
he was equally beloved, he departed from Eyam,
in the year 1790.

On leaving this village where he had spent the
flower of his days, " through evil and good re-
port," he was appointed chaplain to the English
Factory, at Smyrna, where he dwelled several
years. From the time of his leaving Eyam he was
faithfully and almost unremittingly attended by
Misfortune: in the Archipelago he narrowly

* Vide Gentleman's Magazine, July, 1785, page 531.

N

escaped shipwreck; and at Smyrna he was involved in equal peril by fire, in which his papers and manuscripts were wholly consumed.

To Cunningham, a residence at Smyrna was banishment, and he resolved to revisit his native land. Without friends, money, desolate, unknown, and far from home, he returned on foot through Germany on his way to Paris; suffering from fatigue and endless privations. During this long journey, he approached one night, after a day's hard travelling, a large town on the borders of Hungary, when he sat down by the way-side to reflect on his forlorn condition. After having pondered awhile over his misfortunes, he took from his pocket, for the first time, a volume of poetry, which had been presented to him by an English lady, on his departure from Smyrna. A particular poem had been recommended for his perusal by his female friend, and he turned to the page, where he found, "close nestled within the leaves," a note, or order, for fifty pounds: "thus delicately," says Rhodes, "did an amiable woman contrive to administer to the necessities of a stranger in a foreign land."

To his own country he soon arrived, and undertook the duties of an humble curacy in the vicinity of London, but soon after obtained a small living through the influence of the Devonshire family. This he did not long enjoy. "Invited to preach to a society to whom he had become endeared, at Islington, he attended, and after delivering his last, and one of his best discourses, he dined with the delighted members. He appeared in high spirits, but as soon as the cloth was drawn, while conversing with a gentleman near him, he fell back in his chair, and expired without a sigh or groan:

such was the end of Cunningham." Of his moral
character, during the latter part of his ministry at
Eyam, much has been said: whether justly or not,
I am not able to say. One thing is certain, that
for a great number of years, he was unparralleled
in the fulfilment of his duties; and that he laboured
assiduously to improve the condition of his parishioners, by bettering their manners, and giving in-
struction to youth, wholly regardless of pecuniary
compensation. And did he then fall off from so
noble a duty? If so, how lamentable! Perhaps
he was, to some degree, deteriorated in character
by that vile fiend—foul *slander*,

" Whose head is sharper than the sword, whose tongue
Out-venoms all the worms of *Nile*, whose breath
Rides on the posting winds, and doth belie
All corners of the world. Kings, Queens, and states,
Maids, matrons, nay the secrets of the grave,
This viperous *slander* enters."—CYMBELINE.

In the person of RICHARD FURNESS, Eyam, his
birth-place, furnishes another candidate for literary
honours. In a history of his native village, he
must have a first place as regards literary distinction; and also as respects his having contributed
so very largely towards raising the humble place of
his birth to a classical ascendancy—great among
the villages of the Peak. He is now living in the
vicinity of Sheffield; highly honoured by the
literati of the surrounding country: and, although
declining in years, it is ardently hoped that
his hours are, to some degree, still spent with
the Muses.

Of his poetical works, little need to be said:
they are pretty generally known and commended.
" The Rag-Bag," with the exception of a few fugitive pieces, was his first published work; and by a

many much admired. "Medicus Magus," his
next work is, although not so popular, a far better
written poem. In the latter there are a many
beautiful passages: some novel ideas, highly
characteristic of a fine genius. As this work, consisting of thrée cantos, is on a purely local subject,
it is not, therefore, so generally read, as the former
work; yet there are beauties scattered over the
pages of the latter, highly and intellectually pleasing. Those who have not read "Medicus Magus"
may see a fine passage or two from its pages, quoted
in the foregoing account of the plague; and the
subjoined extract from the same production, if not
of equal merit, is very good:

> "With pleasure man's not uniformly blest,
> Such long satiety would spoil the zest;
> Nor are the sufferings of his nature vain,
> His sweetest moments are the fruits of pain;
> And as the knife a sounder healing brings,
> So virtue's fountain in affliction springs.
> The storms of life all human peace assail,
> Or in the capitol or sheltering dale;
> Alike they drive on infancy and years,
> Each eye must weep the appointed cup of tears;
> Or if, or not, God's blessings are abused,
> From pain no mortal, heaven has yet excused:
> It tends alike, the couch of straw and down,
> The' arthritic monarch and rheumatic clown:
> Smites Æsculapius 'midst his stores of health,
> And batters Crœsus through his walls of wealth."

This ardent votary of the Muses is now fast ad-
vancing on his way through "this vale of tears;"
yet it is fervently hoped that, ere "his sands of
life are run," he will add full many a jewel to his
well-won crown of fame: thus embalming his
memory in the admiration of future times, and em-
blazoning with honour and glory, his loved and
native village—Eyam.

This romantic village has other, if less successful, candidates for poetic honours: and of this class there are a few whose effusions have only been perused by friends.

FAMILIES OF DISTINCTION. There appears to have been but very few families of wealth at Eyam in times of yore. The Staffords were by far the most conspicuous and wealthy. Nothing, however, is known of their lineage; they were exceeding rich, and of great import in the village and neighbourhood. Humphrey, the last male heir of this family, died at Eyam, where they had invariably resided, somewhere about the year A.D. 1580. His immense property was valued at the time of his death, at £400,000, which was equally divided amongst his four daughters. Catherine, the eldest, married Rowland Morewood, of the Oaks, near Bradfield, Yorkshire: she was buried at Bradfield, July 16th, 1595. Gertrude married Rowland Eyre, Esq., Hassop, an ancestor of the present Earl Newburgh: her burial, at Longstone, in A.D. 1624, is recorded on a brass plate in the Church. Ann married Francis Bradshaw, of Bradshaw, near Chapel-en-le-Frith; and the other remaining daughter was, I imagine, never married, but was known as Madame Stafford. Francis Bradshaw had the family mansion of the Staffords included in his wife's share of her father's property, where he and his descendants resided until the plague broke out in Eyam. The house was very capacious and antique; it stood at the west end of Eyam, and a large field, now called the Orchard, and another, the Hall-yard, were its appendages. The fish-pan belonging to this very old mansion was destroyed not many years ago. The last Bradshaw who resided at Eyam, was erecting on the site of the old dwelling, what is now known as the Old Hall, at the very time the plague commenced, when he and his family fled to Brampton, in Yorkshire, and never returned. The new mansion, which was rather elegant, was never finished; three or four families have, however, resided in it some time back, but it is now converted into a barn. On the south front, there is a circular stone containing the crest of the arms of the Bradshaw: *a Hart on a wreath standing under a vine.* The other part of the arms of this family is, *two bendlets between two martlets.** That portion of the Eyam estate belonging to the Bradshaws remained in their family until the death of George Bradshaw, of Bradshaw, the last male heir of the elder branch of the Bradshaws; he left no issue, and his whole property was inherited by his sister Elizabeth, who married Joshua Galliard, Esq., of Edmonton, in Middlesex, by whom she had two sons, Peirce and John; the latter of whom died young. Peirce had a son, Bradshaw Galliard, a poet, and two daughters, Anne and Mary. Anne married Eaglesfield Smith, of Longshaw, Dumfries, Scotland; Mary married Charles Bowles, of Ratcliff, Middlesex, between whom, at the death of Bradshaw Galliard, the whole property of the Bradshaws, was divided. Eaglesfield Smith inherited the Eyam estate. The Morewood property at Eyam was sold in small lots about forty years since.

The Colyns were a family of distinction at Eyam in the reign of Henry the Sixth; but of their descendants and property nothing is now known,

* The notorious Judge Bradshaw was of this family; his grandfather went from Bradshaw Hall, Chapel-en-le-Frith, to Wybersleigh, near Marples, Cheshire, where the regicide was born.

French was the name of another rather important family in the village. A notice of this family is in the Register as follows: " Stephen, the son of Stephen French, baptized Dec. 4th, 1643." The name occurs also amongst those who died of the plague. The Brays were a family of some note at Eyam; the Register has the following record:— " Mr. Bray buried 1640." The Wilsons of Eyam were once a family of substance; in Glover's History of Derbyshire there is this notice: " Richard Milnes, Chesterfield, married Elizabeth, daughter and co-heir of the Rev. R. Wilson, of Burton, Norfolk, and of Eyam, Derbyshire; she died Jan. 17, 1691." The Gibels of Eyam were a family of distinction—the only remains of whom, in Eyam, is their name as distinguishing a barn and a tor: " *Gibel barn,*" and " *Gibel Torr.*"*

Eyam has been the birth place of a few very eccentric characters; amongst whom is one MICHAEL BARBER, who was Parish Clerk 59 years. He was a very learned man in his time— a profound astrologer; and the following anecdote is still related of him:—A villager and Michael were walking one day down Hunger-hill lane, Eyam, when they observed two teams ploughing in an adjoining field. The villager said, " Now, Michael, if you can stop yon two teams I shall have faith in your knowledge and power." Michael immediately went to work in the lane, and succeeded, after having performed certain incantations, in stopping one of the teams, but the other kept on. " There," said Michael, " I have stopped one, but the other I cannot stop." " How is that?"

---

* I have a notion that the Gibels were Colyns—Gibel I cannot find written, and therefore think it is not rightly written here, but it is pronounced now nearly as I have given it.

the villager replied. " Because," said Michael, " the ploughman has said his prayers this morning, and I have no power over those who live in the fear of God." Michael lived to a good old age : he died soon after the plague. Thomas Barber, his son, was also an adept in astrology.

CORNELIUS BRUSHFIELD, of the Hanging-flat, Eyam, was perhaps the greatest anchorite that ever lived. He dwelled in a house built on the ledge of a rock in the Dale, a full quarter of a mile from any other dwelling; and, it is said, that only on one solitary occasion did he leave his abode during his whole life; and this occasion was the great contested election in North Derbyshire, by Harper and Clarke, when Cornelius visited Eyam. He died in 1780, aged 66 years. His family were Presbyterians, and remarkable for their hospitality —never suffering a visitor to leave their house without having first partaken of a basin of milk and some bread.

JOHN GREGORY, of Riley, Eyam, was in his lifetime a very singular character. His contempt of modern habits, patriarchal appearance, and profound knowledge of the most abstruse sciences, rendered him deeply interesting. In his diet, and, in fact, in his whole demeanour, he approached to what may be supposed to have characterized the primitive inhabitants of the world. His apothegms are still current in Eyam. He died greatly venerated June 9th, 1820, aged 70 years.

JOHN DOOLEY, although not eccentric in habits, was still a singular man. His love of music, and astonishing powers of memory, claimed for him general respect and esteem. Perhaps but few individuals ever possessed a greater turn for keen and caustic satire; some of his witty and pithy

remarks will ever be remembered. He died a few
years since at a good old age.

PHILIP SHELDON, in his day, was considered to
be a very singular and disaffected character : time
has, however, proved to every inhabitant of the
village that his singularity consisted in clearly seeing, and in boldly and openly declaring the disas-
trous consequences which would ensue from the
blind policy of our rulers during the last great war
with France. He died in May, 1820.

THOMAS BIRDS, Esq., the well known antiquary
of Eyam, had perhaps the greatest and best collection of fossils and other curiosities in the kingdom; and their dispersion at his death has been
the source of regret to the whole village. He was
greatly distinguished for urbanity; and his benefactions to the poor have rendered his memory deservedly cherished.

Eyam is singularly distinguished for having few
dissenters. With the exception of a very few
Wesleyan Methodists, the whole population are of
the Established Church. Methodism was, however, very early introduced in Eyam; though I
believe the first promulgaters were in no place
more abused. The first sermon preached in Eyam
by the Methodists was in 1765, by Mr. Matthew
Mayer, of Portwood-hall, near Stockport. The
preacher stationed himself by Furness's barn side ;
but so much hostility was exhibited on this and a
subsequent occasion, that he each time narrowly
escaped with life. The few friends of the preacher
were pelted with brick-bats, mud, stones, and other
missiles, and to such a degree did the infatuated
multitude carry on their opposition, that the
preacher had the ringleaders brought before a magistrate, who bound them in recognizances for their

good behaviour in future. Recourse to the law had not, however, the effect anticipated : the mass of the villagers would not suffer the preachers. to come into the village, and for a many years no effort was again made.   The few converts to the new doctrine repaired to Grindleford Bridge, where the preachers were not molested; in time the number increased, and preaching was again resumed in Eyam, and a chapel was erected at the east end of the village somewhere about 1780. Everett, in his History of Methodism, says, that the then inhabitants of Eyam " were employed in the lead mines, and were a most savage race."

BENEFACTORS OF EYAM.   Some centuries ago, a person now unknown, left for the poor of Eyam, £15, the interest of which to be annually paid on St. Thomas's day.   Dr. Edmund Finch, left £15 for the same purpose, the interest to be paid at the same time.   Mr. James Furness left £5 5s. 0d. to be equally divided amongst ten old widows annually.   Eyam is also included in the many villages receiving the well known Gisbourne charity. Dr. Finch, for the teaching of ten poor children of the parish of Eyam, bequeathed to the school £100, which with £15 left by another person, was laid out in freehold land, called the Long Meadow, near Bradwell, now let for £7 a year. Thomas Middleton, Leam, left £5 a year to the school for the teaching of ten children to read and write; this benefaction is charged on two pieces of land, called the Upper and Under Lowe.   His Grace the Duke of Devonshire, makes an annual donation of £2 2s. 0d. to the school; and £1 10s. 0d. is produced by rental of a small piece of common land allotted to the school.   Mr. James Furness left £2 a year to the Sunday School, which sum

is now equally divided between the school of the
Methodists and that of the Established Church.
Of the latter school, my father was principal master
from its establishment in 1814, to his death in 1832.

The Endowed School is a modern building—
only remarkable for its "cotton-mill-like appearance." Mr. Samuel Bromley is the present
schoolmaster, who is highly and justly respected
for his abilities and morality.

At the present day, Eyam is the residence of a
many respectable families, whose respective dwellings are distinguished by elegance and respecta-
bility. The RECTORY, for its commodiousness,
situation, gardens, and scenery, is not surpassed
by any parsonage house in England. It was re-
built, in an improved style of architecture, about
seventy-five years ago, at the expence of the Rev.
T. Seward, Rector of Eyam. Since then its exterior has been greatly improved, and very much
so by its present occupant, the Rev. E. B. Bagshaw, Rector. EYAM HALL, the residence of P.
Wright, Esq., is a large, handsome, and rather
antique looking building. The architecture is of
the reign of Elizabeth, but it is a comparatively
modern erection—not above a century and a half
old, if so much. I have heard this mansion stated
as being the same in architecture as Hayes' Farm
House, in Devonshire, the house in which Sir
Walter Raleigh was born; it is, however, only in
one or two particulars that there is any similarity.
Eyam Hall is certainly a capacious and massive
building, with exterior appendages quite in keeping with the design of the structure; and I have
heard the present occupant highly commended by
one skilled in architecture, for preserving, as respects the appendages, the uniformity of the whole.

The Wrights are a very ancient and wealthy family, highly distinguished for equability, consideration, and punctuality.   A female of this family married, nearly a century ago, one of the Traffords, of Trafford Hall, Lancashire, who were related through marriage to the Booths, Earls of Warrington.

Eyam Firs, is a secluded and beautiful villa, a little north of the village. It is the residence of John Wright, Esq., the elder brother of P. Wright, Esq., Eyam Hall.

Eyam Terrace, in the east of the village, has been often admired for its picturesque situation. Its contiguity to the Dale, so beautifully romantic, adds infinitely to its delightfulness. It is owned and occupied by Thomas Fentem, Esq., Surgeon, who has inherited much of the property of his maternal grandfather, the late Philip Sheldon, Eyam.

A little south-west of the Church, a substantial and highly finished house, has been of late erected by M. M. Middleton, Esq., Leam Hall. It is occupied by William Wyatt, Esq., late of Foolow.

Eyam View, is a very elegant dwelling at the west-end of the village, belonging to Thomas Burgoine, Esq., Edenzor; and late in the occupation of George Platt, Esq.

The residence of Thomas Gregory, Solicitor, is a very substantial house in the west end of the village.   And a very excellent and handsome villa is now being erected in the Edge, by Mr. Francis Cocker, Eyam.   There are also five good Inns in the village : the Bull's Head, the principal Inn, by Mr. John Booth; the Miners' Arms, by Mr. William Gregory; the Bold Rodney, by Mr. Samuel Furness; the Rose and Crown, by Mr. Verdan Siddall; and the King's Arms, by Mr. John Slinn.

A Society of Miners, or Sick Society, was established in Eyam, A.D. 1767; a Female Sick Society A.D. 1807; a Cow Club A.D. 1838; and a Funeral Club A.D. 1839; nearly all of which are in an improving state. But Eyam has another equally commendable institution—a Subscription Library, containing above 500 volumes, well selected. It was established A.D. 1821, under the auspices of the Hon. and Rev. Robert Eden, Charles Fentem, Esq., Mr. F. Cocker, Mr. J. Froggatt, and Mr. P. Furness. A Mechanics' Institution has also been judiciously thought of—or rather exists in an embryo state.

During the last great struggle with France, Eyam furnished a company of volunteers, about 100 in number, who went together with the Bakewell and Upper Haddon companies, on permanent duty to Ashbourn. The Eyam company were commanded by P. Wright, Esq., Captain; — Carliel, Esq., Major; and John Cooper, Lieutenant. Robert Brushfield was Drill Sergeant; Jonathan Hallam, Corporal; Thomas Hancock, Drummer; and James Fox, Bugle-man and Fifer.

Eyam, though I have invariably designated it as a village, is provincially called a town; and it had formerly a weekly market and an annual fair; both have been long discontinued. Annual horse races were also formerly held on Eyam Moor. The hippodrome, or old race course, and sod huts or booths remained in part until the enclosure of the moor.

Before cart-ways were made in the vicinity of Eyam, all articles were conveyed to and fro by horses with packsaddles, and the driver was called *jagger*. From the necks of the horses bells were suspended, which could be heard at a great distance; always announcing the jagger's return, and

o

creating a smile of joy on the faces of his wife and children.

The Dale, Eyam, the resort of the idle wanderer and the tasteful tourist, furnishes amongst its numerous objects of wonder, a few circumstances of an appalling nature. Nearly a century ago, a boy about sixteen years of age, named Samuel Blackwell, went in haste to obtain some yew to make billets. The yew tree grew on the top of one of the highest rocks in the Dale; and the poor boy in his haste ran down a small declivity to the tree at such a speed, that when there he could not stop himself, but plunged through the branches, to one of which he hung by the heel for a few minutes, and then fell to the bottom, where he was taken up nearly dashed to pieces. The rock is called, to this day, Blackwell's tor.

A little nearer to Middleton, in this singular dale, there is a very extensive cavern, called Caelswark, in which a Scotch pedlar was found murdered, about fifty years since. The unfortunate man was well known; he had regularly attended the villages in the peak with his wares. The occasion of his murder occurred at Eyam: he had legally stopped some parties for selling goods at the wakes-eve, which so enflamed them with anger, that they followed him at night to the Moon Inn, Stoney Middleton, where they, through the connivance of the landlord, strangled and robbed him, and then carried his corpse into this cavern. About twenty years after, his body was found by Peter Merril, Eyam, who had had a remarkable dream on the subject. Nothing was scarcely known of his murder, until his body was found, when it was removed to Eyam Church, where it lay in a box for a many years, before it was buried.

The buckles of his shoes and other articles of his apparel proved it to be the body of the well-known pedlar ; and other circumstances have since transpired in confirmation thereof. The murderers were never brought to justice, although in a great measure known.

Very near the Caelswark is the cavern called the WONDER, which is explored by numberless strangers every year. It was once richly adorned with stalactites of innumerable forms, which have been taken therefrom to the cabinets of the curious. This cavern has communication with others that are said to extend for miles : at least there are fissures, which pass from the dale under Eyam to that extent : and one of them as far as Bradwell. The Lover's-leap is a very high rock in the dale, from which a love-sick maid, Hannah Baddaley, threw herself, but miraculously sustained very little injury. The Rock-garden was once the greatest object of attraction in this romantic dell : it was the repository of all kinds of fossils, found in the Peak ; and their dispersion has been greatly regretted by the inhabitants of Eyam. In this very interesting place is the Merlin—a cavern abounding with wonder ; but it is not so often visited on account of its being at times almost filled with water, which appears to rise from some subterraneous cavity. I cannot think of this water without fancying I see the Proteus anguinus.* The pristine grandeur of this wonderful dale has been destroyed by the burning of lime, which is now carried on there to a great extent.

The tourist may leave this deep and interesting dingle and ascend an eminence on the opposite side of Eyam, and there behold the greatest con-

* Vide Sir H. Davy's posthumous work, " The Last Days of a Philosopher."

trast in scenery. This eminence is called Rock-Hall, whence may be seen the scattered villages in the dim distance, and endless hills shoulder-lifting the clouds. It is said that with a good glass Lincoln Minster may be seen from this place.

On the arrival of the Pretender, at Macclesfield, in A.D. 1745, the villagers of Eyam were thrown into the greatest consternation: they concealed their furniture and valuables in the mines. One man had his furniture and himself let down into a mine in the Pippin; and the clock struck one while hanging in the shaft: " I'feth," said he, "it would go if 'twere hung in an ash tree."

Much might be said respecting the inclosure of the moor, but it would be dry and uninteresting. There was a former inclosure of what was called the main-field; and the fields still called the " New Closes," were the first enclosed. Some common belonging to Longstone was claimed and obtained by Eyam, in consequence of the people of Longstone refusing to bury a woman who was found dead thereon. The parish of Eyam interred the woman, and claimed the common to the place where the body was found.

The Flora, cattle, land, and fossils of Eyam, are much the same in nature and character as those of the Peak in general. In quantity and excellency of water, Eyam has the advantage of almost every village in Derbyshire: and I have heard it frequently stated that there is a hot spring at the bottom of the New Engine climbing shaft, of supposed sanative properties.

> " My task is done; my song hath ceased; my theme
> Has died into an echo."—BYRON.

PRINTED BY WHITAKER AND CO., FARGATE, SHEFFIELD.

CPSIA information can be obtained
at www.ICGtesting.com
Printed in the USA
BVOW06s0933230817
492838BV00028B/243/P